D0250254

JUST AS I AM

David Ring

Eph. 3: 20, 21

David Ring was born in an impoverished town in Arkansas, the youngest of eight children. When he was fourteen, his mother died, and he was passed from family member to family member, never again to feel the love of his mother.

David, a graduate of William Jewel College, is a staff evangelist for First Baptist College, Orlando. He speaks in more than 200 churches a year, and has been a guest on *The Old Time Gospel Hour* and *The 700 Club*.

Lela Gilbert is the author or co-author of more than 30 books. Her love of the arts is apparent through her dedication to writing fiction, nonfiction, children's books, poetry, and music.

269.2092
R581Da

JUST AS I AM

THE LIFE OF
DAVID RING
As told to Lela Gilbert

MOODY PRESS
CHICAGO

82915

© 1993, 1996 by
DAVID RING

All rights reserved. No part of this book may be reproduced in any form without permission in writing from the publisher, except in the case of brief quotations embodied in critical articles or reviews.

All Scripture quotations, unless indicated, are taken from the *New American Standard Bible*, © 1960, 1962, 1963, 1968, 1971, 1972, 1973, 1975, 1977, and 1994 by The Lockman Foundation, La Habra, Calif. Used by permission.

Scripture quotations marked (NIV) are taken from the *Holy Bible: New International Version*® NIV®. Copyright © 1973, 1978, 1984 by International Bible Society. Used by permission of Zondervan Publishing House. All rights reserved.

Scripture quotations marked (KJV) are taken from the King James version of the Bible.

PHOTO CREDITS: Page 7 copyright © 1993 by Christopher Yates Photography. All other photos from David Ring Ministries.

ISBN: 0-8024-1733-7

9 10

Printed in the United States of America

To my loving momma, Leron Ring,
for giving me a chance to live, to survive in this world. With-out your investing your life and love in me I wouldn't have made it. You always looked beyond my imperfect body and saw my needs. Thank you for loving me unconditionally.

To my faithful wife, Karen,
for making an unseen Friend a reality in my life. Your love and support have been a real source of strength, especially during the days when I didn't feel like continuing because of my body's pain. Your faithfulness to our children when they needed a dad has sustained them in my absence. You truly are my best friend.

To my adorable children, April Jane,
Ashley Dawn, Nathan David, and Amy Joy,
for being a daily reminder of God's grace in my life. You are more fun than I dreamed possible. I am very proud of each of you.

CONTENTS

FOREWORD

David Ring is an amazing young man.

His courage in the face of hardship and determination to overcome adversity have been a great inspiration to me. David had every reason to give up on life and accept failure. He experienced the emotional pain of rejection and loss, and he continues to know the pain of physical suffering. He has endured more hardship in his young life than most of us will face in a lifetime. Yet David Ring refuses to be discouraged by the circumstances of life.

If any person in the world has reason to be discouraged or bitter about the life God has given them, David Ring does. But David has risen above these so-called limitations and is accomplishing much for the kingdom of Jesus Christ.

I first met David when he came to Thomas Road Baptist Church as a guest evangelist. The first time David told his life story at Thomas Road Baptist Church, we laughed, we wept, and we watched in amazement as God used this talented young preacher to remind us again that we serve a miracle-working God.

Since then, he has returned to our church many times. When David stands in the pulpit, a noticeable air of anticipation fills the sanctuary. The members of my congregation are expecting a blessing—and when David preaches, they are never disappointed.

His sense of humor and optimism are contagious. As he tells his story, you cannot help but admire this remarkable young man.

God did not work a miracle of physical healing in David's life. He instead chose to take this young man and work a miracle of faith in his life. It is David Ring's faith—his unshakable confidence in God's goodness—that allows him to triumph over what some would consider a devastating physical condition.

David inspires all who hear him and with the publication of this book, I'm certain he will inspire readers everywhere. It is impossible to "experience" David Ring and come way unchanged. When David says, "I have cerebral palsy, what's your problem?" you will be challenged to look beyond the pain of your present circumstances and will be encouraged to go out and serve God as you never have before.

Read the story of his beautiful wife, precious children, and growing ministry—all the things people told him he could never have—and you will find yourself believing again in the God of the impossible. Read the words that have almost become a trademark of David's, "Don't ask why, ask what," and you will be reminded of our purpose in life. God has not put us on this earth to fulfill our own selfish desires. We are here to bring glory to God, however difficult or easy our lives may be.

Just As I Am concludes with the words to David's testimony song, "Victory in Jesus." Those words, and David's firm belief, may well convince you of a profound truth of God's wonder-working power: absolutely nothing is impossible through the power of our Savior, Jesus Christ.

JERRY FALWELL

ACKNOWLEDGMENTS

Several people have been instrumental in making this book a reality. A project like this comes together only with great effort from many dedicated, unselfish people. I am grateful to God for the following behind-the-secenes warriors:

Danny de Armas, the executive director of our ministry. He has worked faithfully in developing this book. Without his leadership, *Just As I Am* would never have become a reality.

Bonnie Kuykendall, my secretary. Your dedication to our ministry is a blessing.

Lela Gilbert. Thank you for using your God-given talents to communicate God's grace on these pages. Thanks for being available to our Lord.

President Joseph Stowell and Tim Ostrander of Moody Bible Institute and Greg Thornton and his wonderful staff at Moody Press for believing in this project and for your untiring efforts in bringing it to pass. What great joy to have worked with you.

Dr. Ben Guedes. I appreciate your contribution to this work and your personal interest in me.

My brothers and sisters who helped me when I was at my weakest point in life. You saw me at my worst and loved me anyway, especially Lameda and her family.

In addition to the above encouragers, I also am grateful to those who thought I couldn't accomplish something. In truth, your discouragement was used by God to help me work hard. I learned to trust God to see the impossible become possible.

Finally, the message of this book and ministry is due to the men of God whom He placed in my life along the way to plant, water, and fertilize so that His work would be accomplished in me. Thanks also to the the hundred of pastors who have welcomed me to their pulpits with this life-changing message of God's grace.

1

AN UNLIKELY MESSENGER

There is a rustling and a moment of curiosity as the pastor and his guest speaker make their way across the platform. By the time the singing ends, the church is packed with worshipers. The minister offers a few words of greeting to the congregation and to the many visitors in attendance. He then introduces the guest speaker.

The sandy-haired man has fair skin, intelligent, blue eyes, and a quick smile. His limp is slightly more noticeable than the shakiness of his hands. When he begins to speak, however, it is obvious that he has difficulty—there is an evident impediment. But soon his handicaps become part of his charm. In fact, David Ring's victorious battle with cerebral palsy is the primary reason people crowd into church sanctuaries all over America to hear him.

David speaks in his own unique dialect, developed through the years, so the words he uses can be pronounced clearly enough to be understood. Even at that, now and then a word or phrase gets past the listener. David is well aware that some words don't come out quite right all the time. So he repeats important statements more than once. By the time he has finished speaking, his listeners have little doubt as to what he wanted to say.

And when David Ring addresses an audience, he is immediately and irresistibly disarming.

Some of you are looking me over. You're looking me up one side and down the other. That's OK. I am looking you over too.

You say, "I don't think I'm going to like you." Well, you don't have any option. The Lord Jesus said to "love one another." You have to love me whether you want to or not.

And I have to love you whether I want to or not. By looking at some of you, I think that's going to be very difficult!

You say, "David, what's wrong with you?" I was born with cerebral palsy. So I talk a little bit different. I don't want that to bother you because it doesn't belong to you. It belongs to me. So leave it alone. I promise you, you cannot catch it. You have to be born with it.

You say, "Preacher, I can't understand you." Well, hang in there. I'm like an old wart. I have to grow on you, and by the time I am finished, I am going to grow all over you!

So the adventure of getting acquainted with David Ring begins. The "handicapped" young man appeals to the "normal" men and women in the congregation to receive the joy of salvation and the strength for living that he has gained from his Christian faith. He implores them to appropriate the strength of his Lord—a "strength made perfect in weakness."

He invites them to give God their worst along with their best so that He can make something beautiful out of the most heartbreaking difficulties.

David Ring stands in pulpits as a living testament to God's incredible power; he calls himself "a trophy of God's grace." He represents the most formidable challenges and complications that life has to offer. He commands attention because he has refused to submit to his troubles, and he has known more troubles than his share—more than nearly anyone who listens, transfixed and often transformed, to the story of his life.

Jonesboro, Arkansas, is an agricultural community, the home of Arkansas State University. Located on the fertile Mississippi Delta, the greater Jonesboro area is made up of flat farmland that is irrigated by many slow, shallow rivers. Cotton and soybean fields stretch across acres of land, watched over by simple, country houses.

In the nineteenth century, the largest recorded earthquake in North American history rumbled through the area, thanks to the massive New Madrid quake fault, which is sixty miles northeast of Jonesboro proper. The possibility of another deadly temblor is not far from residents' minds. Jonesboro is also located in a notorious tornado alley, and precautions against total destruction are part of each citizen's daily life. Late summer inevitably finds the entire vicinity braced for disaster.

It was in the Jonesboro area that Oscar Newton Ring and his wife, Leron, reared their family. As threatening as the potential may have been for community tragedy, the Ring's actual experiences represent unbelievable personal disaster.

In addition to Oscar and Leron's eight surviving children, they bore two who died at birth. Of the eight who lived, all four sons were handicapped. David's three older brothers, Glendale, Bill, and Wilburn, were hemophiliacs. Their blood did not clot, which caused frequent internal bleeding. Even the slightest wound was life endangering, and their mother was forever alert to any imaginable mishap. At one point, because of his hemophilia, Glendale was unable to walk for three years. None of David's brothers is living today; one recently died of AIDS after receiving infected blood during a transfusion.

David's birth in 1953 was marred by ominous complications. He was technically dead for eighteen minutes after delivery, during which time no oxygen reached his brain. By the time life was finally breathed into him, his brain was permanently damaged by cerebral palsy.

Dr. Ben Guedes, an Orlando pediatrician who specializes in cerebral palsy, explains the condition and the way it affects David.

> Cerebral palsy is defined as any central motor deficit presumed to be caused by events in the perinatal or prenatal period. In layman's language, this means that it is a brain injury affecting neuromuscular control. The injury could occur *in utero* or in the events surrounding birth, as was the case with David Ring. Although frequently associated with mental retardation, cerebral palsy is defined as a primary motor disorder, and mental retardation is not necessarily present. C.P. is also defined as nonprogressive. In other words, the injury does not grow or spread.
>
> David Ring has a form of spastic cerebral palsy, which is identified by stiffness of extremities and difficult movement due to chronic "tightness" of [adjacent] muscle groups.
>
> The outlook of C.P. patients depends on the severity of the handicaps and the acceptance and nurturing of caregivers. In addition, of course, therapy may be helpful depending on the nature of the problem. As long as intellectual capacity is normal, adjustment can frequently be made for severe handicaps. As the person matures, the tendency is for [contracting] of joints and loss of use of extremities to occur; however, an equilibrium is usually reached in which stability of disability occurs for many years.

As far as life-span is concerned, it is highly variable.
. . . There is not a lot written about people of David's age
with his particular constellation of symptoms. I think it is safe
to say that the longstanding abnormal muscle tension from
spasticity will take its toll on joints and general energy level.
Pain due to arthritis or other joint problems will likely be a
more common feature. It will be important for David to remain active and, probably, under the care of a rheumatologist
to maintain function as long as possible.

As Dr. Guedes writes, "The outlook depends on the se-
verity of the handicaps and the acceptance and nurturing of
caregivers." In David's case, the handicaps were quite severe.
But David's primary caretaker, his mother, was remarkably
accepting and nurturing. Had it not been for her devotion to
him, his story might have been far different.

David often reminds his listeners of how easy it could
have been for the mother of three disabled youngsters to
choose to abort a pregnancy—a difficult one that came "too
late" in life. Having seen David's condition, how simple it
might have been to institutionalize the infant, so great would be
his demand upon her time and energy. But neither alternative
occurred to Leron Ring. Love was the only option she knew.

Leron was not a sophisticated woman by any stretch of
the imagination. She was no theologian, nor was she an ex-
pert on "the family." She was the wife of a country preacher
and farmer, quite unaware of modern psychological theory.
Tall, stocky, and proud to say that she was as strong as a man,
Leron was a jolly woman. She loved to laugh and was always
the life of the party, delighting the people around her with
her humor and her love of practical jokes.

Most significant, Leron Ring's heart was full of affection
for her children. She had the unique ability to cherish her disabled son David as if he were the most important person in the
world. With a firm foundation of confidence and courage, she
prepared David for the public life he would eventually lead.

In those early years, the entire family accepted their crippled younger brother without apology. All of his siblings but one were much older than David, and several of them were married with children older than he was. David's siblings played with him, taught him, and encouraged him to be himself. In spite of his physical difficulties, he was a happy child who was deeply bonded to his mother. Leron was always there to wipe away his tears of frustration. She was at hand to help him accomplish the tasks that were too hard for his small, shaky fingers. And Leron was quick to remind the boy that she loved him—countless times every day.

Trapped in a body that caused him to experience unbelievably insecure feelings, David Ring nevertheless felt emotionally protected as long as his mother was around. Leron and her husband worked hard to eke out sustenance for their large family, but there was no shortage of affection as far as David was concerned. He likes to remember those happy times.

"I used to sit on my momma's lap to watch TV," David recalls. "I used to go to the store with my precious momma. There was something about being in my momma's arms. I felt secure. I felt warm. I felt loved. I remember at night when I used to go to bed, I would never crawl between the sheets without putting a kiss on my momma's face. I remember that when my momma said, 'David, my little baby boy, I love you today!' my little heart would melt. I knew everything was OK, because my momma knew me. My momma loved me, even though I had a shaky body. My momma still loved me, and that's what counted."

David's early school years were surprisingly unmarred by cruelty. There were pressures, to be sure. David struggled with coordination, and his efforts to write and speak and eat were never-ending. But in Jonesboro, David Ring was just "one of the bunch." That was, no doubt, because he was always surrounded by the same people—people who had known and accepted him all his life.

Of course, life wasn't always easy. He recalls one particular incident that epitomized his childhood challenges. Though he wasn't the greatest ball player in the school, David enjoyed trying, and his classmates were happy to include him on their teams. One day during fourth grade, he was hurrying to complete a math exam so he could go out and play baseball with the other kids.

Everyone had filed out for recess. Although he was a straight-A student in math, David needed a long time to do his work. He struggled to write out his answers as quickly as his shaky hands would allow him; he couldn't go to the playground until his test was finished. All at once the bell startled him—the bell announcing that recess was over.

The other kids strolled back into class, laughing and talking about their ball game. David took one look at them, and frustration suddenly overwhelmed him. He burst into tears. *Why was life so hard?*

His teacher enfolded the heartbroken little boy in her arms. "David, it's OK. It's OK."

But it wasn't OK. Did anyone understand how difficult life was for him? Only his mother seemed to know.

The school called Leron, and she rushed over to pick David up. Once they were in the car driving home, she took her son's hand in hers. His tears started again, along with an outburst of emotion.

"Why, Momma, why? Why do I shake? Why can't I finish a math test? Why can't I play on the playground with the other kids? Why am I different from the other kids? Why, Momma? Why? Why?"

"David, my little baby boy," she said softly. As well as she could, Leron tried to explain his crippling condition. David didn't understand a great deal. But one thing he knew—he was different from the other children. Never before that day had he felt that difference so strongly.

David's father, Oscar Ring, was a rangy, six-foot man with weather-beaten skin and brown eyes. All his life Oscar had toiled in the Arkansas fields, struggling to feed the hungry mouths of his growing family. His daily life was grueling, but he earned the respect of his community by his godliness and strength of character.

Oscar was a quiet man who kept his thoughts to himself. He deeply loved his children, and they returned his love spontaneously. In 1942, Oscar felt called of God to become a preacher. He began to speak in his local church and in the surrounding communities. In 1945 he lost one arm in a cotton gin accident; yet he continued to labor in both vocations, while instilling values in his children that they would never forget.

Despite the family's commitment to the Lord and to His Word, difficulties between David's parents arose in the early 1960s. They had left the farm and moved into the town of Jonesboro. David also found the change difficult. Accustomed to the farm where he could not see another house for miles, he now lived in a neighborhood, with houses side by side. At first the family took shelter in a church there, trying to get situated in a new environment.

It wasn't easy for a pair of cotton and soybean farmers to find employment in town. Eventually, Leron got a job in the cafeteria at Arkansas State University. Oscar continued his preaching and began to work as a janitor in the school's gymnasium. Sometimes David accompanied his dad as he set up the bleachers, goals, and equipment for university basketball games.

Once the family found a house on the college campus, David was enrolled in elementary school. At one point school officials tried to place him in a handicapped class. The idea was short-lived, however; he was far too bright to struggle along with the other less gifted students. His mind was sound; only his body was uncooperative, and even his physical skills astonished people now and then.

For instance, David wanted to ride a bicycle. Leron and the rest of his family discouraged David from trying; they feared for his safety. But David was determined to learn, even though maintaining his balance was especially hard for him. He secretly took a bike out to the hill behind his house. Although not very high, the hill seemed huge to the little boy. He got onto the bike and started riding.

He shook a little, but he told himself, *You have two options: you can fall, get hurt, and maybe break your neck, or you can keep on going.* He continued to pedal and made it to the bottom without falling once.

Once David decided to climb into a motorized go-cart that some neighborhood children had built. He watched closely as each child took a turn driving it. When David's turn came, no one but David himself was sure what would happen. They should have guessed—he simply sat down, pulled away from the curb, and steered the car as well as everyone else had. It wasn't the last time David Ring would amaze onlookers with his ability to drive. Years later, he bewildered his adult friends by getting a driver's license.

Although those childhood days were pleasant enough for David, all was not well between his mother and father. Their ceaseless struggle for survival had taken a fearful, and eventually fateful, toll on their marital relationship. After several exceptionally stressful months in Jonesboro, Oscar and Leron went their separate ways. They lived apart until Oscar's unexpected death two years later, yet another tragedy that afflicted the Rings. David was only eleven when his father died from liver cancer. He remains confident, though, that his dad is "with the Lord."

"Having gone to church all my life, I know the Bible says that when you die in the Lord you are going to be with the Lord and live with the Lord forever and forever. I know that my daddy is up in heaven today having a good time with Jesus, because the Bible says, 'To be absent from the body is to be present with the Lord.'

"I can't wait. I can't wait to go up to my daddy in heaven and say, 'Daddy, thank you for loving me.

'Thank you, Daddy, for preaching the Word.

'Thank you, Daddy, that when you lost your arm, you were trying to make a living for your family.

'Thank you, Daddy, for not putting down the Word of God.

'Thank you, Daddy, for being known in northeast Arkansas as the one-armed preacher man.

'Thank you, Daddy, for setting an example for your little baby boy.'

"Many times I wonder, *What would Daddy think of me? Do I hold the Word of God high like my daddy? I wonder, Daddy, are you proud of me? What do you think, Daddy?*"

The Ring family's life story was catastrophic. Oscar's mangled arm. The death of two infants. Three hemophiliacs. David's cerebral palsy. The Rings' broken marriage. Oscar's premature death. The ongoing assault of poverty that never abated. It was a life that could have broken the heart of a weaker woman than Leron Ring. It nearly broke her spirit—but it didn't.

After her divorce from Oscar, Leron remarried. For a while she wandered away from the things she had always believed in. She stopped going to church. Her friendship with the Lord became estranged. She ceased praying. She stopped singing the hymns she loved. She no longer felt God's presence. Then one Sunday night she found her way to the altar of Macedonia Baptist Church. With tears of repentance, she asked God to forgive her for drifting away from Him.

David watched his mother make that long and humbling trek down the aisle. He felt every step as if he were taking it with her. *What will people think?* He watched, breathless, to see what the congregation's response would be. *Will they mock or criticize her?* It wasn't long before waves of love swept away all his fears. Almost as one, the church people opened their arms to embrace Leron. They welcomed her back tearfully. They rejoiced wholeheartedly with her as she rededicated her life to the Lord.

That scene was imprinted on young David's heart, and it would serve him well in the future. That joyful event in Leron's life encouraged his heart years later when, recalling his mother's courage, David was able to make his own similar journey toward an altar.

Leron Ring could not have survived without the joy of the Lord in her heart because "the joy of the Lord was her strength." She wasn't happy all the time—and couldn't have been. She wasn't a stranger to sin, and she knew the bitter taste of failure. But Leron knew real joy, and she taught her youngest son its immeasurable value. Today, when he speaks to crowds, David likes to talk about true joy.

If you want joy, real joy, wonderful joy, let Jesus come into your heart.

Every child of God receives joy at the time of his new birth. The second trait of the Spirit is joy, according to Galatians 5:22.

I'm not talking about happiness. Happiness and joy are totally different. Happiness comes and goes, but joy comes and stays.

Getting married, dating, having children, driving, getting good grades, receiving a raise or a job promotion, or buying a new house may make people happy. Even the world has its "Happy Hour." Happiness is determined by circumstances, but joy depends on our relationship with the Lord Jesus. Your happiness can be taken away because of circumstances, but nobody can remove your joy.

You say, "Dave, I'm saved, but I don't think I have joy." Do you know why? It is because circumstances are robbing you of the joy that is in you. Joy is still inside you, but the problem is that someone or something is stifling your joy. Joy should be an outward expression of an inward experience.

After he sinned, King David said, "Lord, restore unto me the joy of Thy salvation." It is my prayer that we start bubbling over with joy unspeakable to a lost and unhappy world.

The message of exchanging sin for the hope and joy of salvation is never far from David Ring's thoughts. He saw his father preach it; he saw his mother live it. And today he sees hope for the person who seeks the Lord in humility and brokenness. His own metamorphosis from a "lonely little crippled boy," as he once saw himself, to a nationally acclaimed spokesman for the Christian gospel reminds him every day that "all things are possible."

As far as David Ring is concerned, those infinite possibilities begin at the cross of Jesus Christ. He knows and speaks about the cross because he has been there.

The journey David took to the foot of that cross was not an easy one. It was marked by heartbreak and rejection, both for David and for those who tried to help him along the way.

2

A SEASON
OF LOSSES

As he travels around America speaking in churches and at other gatherings, David Ring preaches a sermon titled "Thou Shalt Not Bellyache." He bases it on a text from the New Testament, excerpted from Paul's first letter to the Thessalonians, chapter 5, verse 18: "In everything give thanks," the texts reads, "for this is God's will for you in Christ Jesus."

David explains the reason for his unusual sermon title.

You say, "How did you ever come up with the subject of bellyaching?"

One day as I was contemplating that the church needs revival today, I realized that one reason we don't experience it is because we bellyache. We complain the majority of the

*time. We miss out on much of God's best because of our
complaining about things in our lives.*

*The children of Israel wandered around in the wilder-
ness for forty years because of their murmuring. They were
not grateful to God for what they had. The people who were
delivered out of Egypt did not get to experience personal revival or God's Promised Land. They missed out on God's
milk and honey because of their ungrateful hearts.*

*I wonder how many of us are missing our own Promised
Land daily because we are not giving thanks for everything in
our lives. Until we learn to give thanks in everything, we will
not be in the will of God. Therefore, we won't have revival in
our lives, church, and land.*

What is the will of God?

In everything give thanks.

In the good times, thank God for everything.

In the bad times, thank God for everything.

*Because the Bible says this is the will of God in Christ
Jesus concerning you.*

If ever a man had reason to complain, to bemoan his
state, to "bellyache," David Ring had a reason. His life has
been a continuous struggle against adversity since birth. The
moment he entered the world, he had to fight for breath, and
that was only the beginning.

Yet today he is a jovial person who always has an encouraging word for his companions. He proudly passes out
T-shirts imprinted "Don't Whine, But Shine!"—words that
clearly express his personal credo. Though he is known as an
evangelist, David Ring is much more. He is a motivator. He
is an adamant spokesman for positive self-esteem. He is an
overcomer who has done everything he was not supposed to
be able to do.

A man with a speech impediment should not be preaching 250 times a year.

A man with cerebral palsy should not be married to a lovely, devoted wife or be the father of four delightful children.

A man with coordination problems should not be driving a car on the highway.

For that matter, many victims of cerebral palsy don't live past thirty years of age. David Ring is moving into his forties with reasonable health and comfort.

An observer asks what kind of travail must have been necessary for David to accomplish so many all-but-impossible tasks. Speaking is clearly difficult for him. Eating is laborious. Actions that most people do without thinking have to be planned carefully and undertaken to conserve the most possible energy. Nothing is easy for him.

So what happened to give this man such an edge on attitude? Has he always had his "Give thanks in all things" point of view? A look at David Ring's life answers those questions clearly.

He has not always looked at life victoriously. In fact, David probably experienced one of the most devastating periods of adolescent transition imaginable. During those dark years, he was the last person on earth who wanted to hear about "positive thinking." One thing remained constant, though: his mother's love. But he was about to be threatened with her loss, too.

"I love my momma. I'm not only the baby of the family, but I'm an A Number One momma's boy. You can tell by looking at me that I'm a momma's boy, because I got that momma baby face.

"Every morning when my momma and I got up, we put our arms around each other, and we told each other we loved each other. In those moments I felt secure and warm. I received my strength for the daily activities that were about to come. Momma protected me. Momma seemed to make everything right in my life. When I was in my momma's arms, I didn't have a care in the world. Nothing is wrong with loving your momma. I think everybody needs a momma's love; everybody needs a momma's touch.

"Today I know why it is so important to tell our Lord we love Him daily. When we do, we receive our daily strength to face life's struggle. He seems to make everything all right. Even though humanly speaking everything is caving in on us, we feel secure in the arms of our Savior. Our only real security is in Jesus. Everything else in our lives is only a vapor. One day we have it, and the next we don't.

"I learned that lesson the hard way. One day when I was fourteen, my momma got sick. The woman I loved and adored, the woman I rose up every morning and called blessed—she went into the hospital and had an operation on her neck the day before Mother's Day, 1968. A simple operation, we thought.

"In July, two months later, the doctors came to my family and said, 'Your momma will never come home again. She has cancer. She has six months, at the very most, to live.'"

Once again, the Ring family seemed to be targeted for tragedy. Their battle for stability and success had always been hard fought, and now another ruinous blow seemed to be at hand. The courageous woman who had held her family together with fortitude and courage began to wither.

Leron Ring had already experienced a bout with breast cancer, which had alarmed the family four years earlier. But, characteristically, she had defeated it with her usual spunk. More recently, a lump on her neck had sent her to the doctor, and the doctor had dispatched her to the hospital immediately. She returned home after the surgery, to everyone's relief. But two months later she was hospitalized again, and the doctors did not expect her to return home.

David was living outside Jonesboro when two of his sisters told him the news. Janice, who was closest to his age, had been his best friend throughout his life. She and Lameda, an older sister from Missouri, sat the boy down and began to explain the harsh facts to him. David describes his response.

"I did the only thing I knew to do. I got down on my knees every day, every night, and I said, 'God, please don't take my momma. God, please don't take my momma. God, please don't take my momma. God, my momma is the only thing I have. God, don't take my momma, please.'"

Leron had been sick for several months. Puberty is a time of emotional struggle for most boys and girls, and David was no exception. His body was changing; his voice was cracking. Those things were to be expected and could be taken in stride—as long as he had his mother's unflagging support and encouragement.

Now that was about to change. Not only was David's mother ill, but he would have to leave Arkansas and go to St. Charles, Missouri, a suburb of St. Louis. His sister Benetta and her husband, Wayne, lived there and had agreed to make room for David in their home. No one, least of all David, realized the impact that such upheaval would have on his young life.

A new home. A new school. New classmates who didn't know him. He had to face everything without the protection and provision of his mother, who had virtually buffered him from pain for his entire lifetime. David's move to Missouri was more traumatic than anyone had expected. Janice had gone to live with a grown brother, Bill, in Paragould, Arkansas. David not only missed his mother painfully, but now he was also removed from Janice, his sister, best friend, and constant companion. The packing and moving and uprooting was difficult enough. But separation from the two people he counted on most in the world sent David into a downhill emotional cycle that continued, unrelieved, for more than a year.

Benetta was David's eldest sister, and she appeared to have a stable home in St. Charles, Missouri, so the Rings had determined that David would be best cared for there. At first there were new experiences that he enjoyed. Little things delighted him. For example, he had had little occasion to eat out in restaurants in Arkansas. However, Benetta and Wayne's family ate out every Friday night, and that was a great treat for David.

But attending the huge school in St. Charles was another matter. David's school in Arkansas had enrolled only five hundred people, ranging from kindergarten through senior high. When David faced difficulties in Jonesboro, his mother had always been there to comfort and defend him.

That was not the case in St. Charles. St. Charles High School had 1,200 students of high school age alone. Not one of them had ever seen David Ring before.

As David recalls about his life with Benetta and her family, "They gave me everything they could, but they couldn't give me the love, and they couldn't give me the joy, and they couldn't give me the touch that only a mom could give me.

"Everywhere I went somebody would point a finger and say, 'Look, that boy walks funny," or, "Look, that boy can't do anything right.'

"It was tough because it was a big school. The building alone was humongous—the campus, the property, all the school buses going early in the morning to the middle of the afternoon. I cannot remember meeting one friend in St. Charles High School."

And so David retreated into a shell. "I couldn't wait until the school day was over to get home to my haven of rest because I was protected there. I tried to work in the school library. They had another handicapped boy there, and they tried to put me in the library to meet people, but I totally rejected that.

"I hated people, because I was really hurt."

Greater than any other obstacle David Ring faced in those transitional months was the deteriorating health of his beloved mother. Every weekend Benetta and Wayne, their daughter Vicki, and David drove to Jonesboro to visit Leron. In a week's time, the change in Leron's condition could be startling. It frightened David more than anything he'd ever faced in his young life. The hospital itself became formidable, as if it were a prison holding captive the one person in the world who could make things right for him.

"I remember how Momma went downhill fast in five days," David says. "Her eyes were sunken, her face was sunken—she was just a skeleton. I never will forget my feelings walking into a 'death room' for the first time. I could feel death in the room.

"Momma was a vibrant, jolly, laughing, person—the life of the party. But when I walked in and saw her, the room was very, very dim, and a brand-new woman was lying there.

"I saw my momma go from 185 pounds to 57 pounds. It tore me up. I didn't want to live. I wanted to die. It devastated me. I thought, *That's not Momma!*"

While Leron lingered between life and death, David continued to appeal to heaven on her behalf. Part of him knew she would never return from the hospital alive. Yet another part of him could not stop pleading with God. Surely a loving heavenly Father would not deprive him of his sole emotional and spiritual support!

The trips to Jonesboro grew increasingly depressing for all the children, and David remembers his last visit to his mother's bedside.

"Just before Momma went to be with the Lord, she was so weak she couldn't even lift a finger. She couldn't even talk above a whisper, because big sores were in her mouth and on her tongue. There's no pain like watching your momma die a slow death.

"The day before my momma went to be with the Lord, though, she became happy in the Lord. She started singing and shouting and praying. Everybody tried to calm Momma down, but when you're happy in the Lord, you don't calm down too easily.

"Finally, forty-five minutes later my momma calmed down, and she said, "Doctor, Doctor! Call my family. I'm going home.""

The family rushed to Jonesboro in response to a phone call from Lameda. Of course, Leron Ring's faith sustained them all—they knew she was heaven-bound, and the older children recognized that her suffering was about to end. Their loss would surely be her gain.

But David's perception was not as selfless. He could not imagine living the rest of his life without his mother. She had surrounded him with comfort. She had filled his world with hope. When necessary, she had carried him, both physically and emotionally.

Everyone gathered around Leron's bed one by one, and each told her good-bye.

"They saved me for last," David says. When he arrived, his mother was semiconcious.

"When it was my turn, I put my head on my momma's chest, and I said, 'Momma, Momma, it's me, your little baby boy.'

"She didn't respond to me. Oh, that broke my heart. My momma always responded to me, but not that time.

"Ten minutes later, I said one more time, 'Momma, Momma, it's me, your little baby boy.'"

Finally her eyes opened, and she saw David. She broke into a big grin, and tears began to roll down her cheeks.

"Dave, my little baby boy," she said, "let me tell you what happened to me today. Today I got happy in Jesus. I saw your daddy, and I saw Jesus standing over on the other side of Jordan's stormy banks with arms wide open, saying, 'Come on home, come on home!'

"David, I don't want to go. I don't want to leave you. But they want me to come on home, and before I leave you, let me tell you one thing. I love you. I really love you."

That's the last thing his momma said to David: "I love you."

His mother then slipped into a deep coma, and Friday evening through Sunday the family spent the weekend there, thinking Momma might die at any time. They finally returned home late Sunday night as Momma clung to life. Leron "crossed Jordan" early Tuesday morning. Benetta and Wayne didn't wake David to tell him the news until the time he normally got up to go to school.

"I will never forget that empty experience as I opened my eyes and saw them standing in the doorway," David says. "Tears were in Benetta's eyes as she said the most painful words that I could hear: 'She's gone.' My heart broke for the final time because I knew that all my hope was gone. My dreams were gone. In fact, my whole life was gone. I remember thinking that dreadful morning, *My purpose for living is gone.*

Instead of enduring another painful day at St. Charles High, David went to his brother Glendale's home in Jonesboro. The funeral arrangements would be made from there.

"It was an empty trip. I thought, *What am I going to do now?* At first it was a shock, but during those four hours (it seemed like four days) reality hit me hard. I cried all the way. Heaven was not a reality for me. I kept thinking over and over, *She's gone. She's gone. She's finally gone. My precious, lovely momma is gone.* It was almost unbearable for me."

Macedonia Baptist Church in Jonesboro was the site of the memorial service.

"The church was filled to overflowing. As we were leaving the auditorium, it hit me again. *She's gone.* On the front porch of that church I thought, *I am saying good-bye for the last time to the woman who invested her life in me. The one who gave me comfort and strength. It's over! How can life go on? Especially mine?*"

David wanted "life to stop so badly." And he admits he "cried buckets of tears on that front porch."

Several of David's old school friends from Jonesboro attended the funeral, providing him with much needed companionship on that worst of days. One particular boy named Freddie Thornton rode with David to Pine Log Cemetery where Leron was laid to rest beside Oscar Ring. There, too, was buried a big part of David's heart.

"Maybe Momma was laid to rest, but I sure wasn't. It was the beginning of the two loneliest years of my life—years of turmoil. Later I recalled that my momma had tried to prepare me for that particular day. One day she took me to town alone. On the way, she looked down at me as she drove and said, 'Dave, what would you do if I were to leave you?'

"I replied, 'What do you mean, Momma?'

"She asked the question again. 'What would you do if I were to leave you?'

"I said, 'Aw, Mom, you are not going to leave me! You're strong. You are not going to leave me! Are you?'

"Little did I know that she was trying to prepare me for what was to come. But she couldn't. You can never prepare a person for as great a loss as that."

Anger did not begin to stir inside David at first—his heartache was so great that he could feel nothing but pain. It did not occur to him in those first days after Leron's death that God had let him down. It was later, in the weeks to come, that he began to rage at the Almighty for not hearing his pleas for mercy. Even Leron herself was not exempt from his bitterness. As children often do, David felt that his mother had abandoned him by dying.

Without his mother and without the presence of God in his life, David found his world descending into utter darkness. He stopped communicating. He stopped trying. He stopped going to school. He lost all hope, all interest, and one by one, his brothers and sisters began to lose interest in him.

One Saturday in late December 1968, David's brother Wilburn and Benetta's husband, Wayne, took David to an A&W Root Beer® stand in a small town outside St. Charles. He sensed tension in their manner as they struggled to inform him of new plans—plans that would once again uproot and unsettle him.

"You're going to have to move out of our house, Dave," Wayne explained. "You'll have to stay away from now on. Benetta just can't handle you anymore."

"Why?" was the only question David could ask. No answer was forthcoming. Naturally, he blamed himself. His young mind raced—had he become that difficult to live with? Was his handicap so unbearable to the people around him? Was he really that unlovable?

Looking up at them, he mumbled, "What about my clothes? My stuff?"

As they were talking, Benetta was packing his things into boxes, and he found them stacked under the carport when they returned to the house. She didn't even come out to say good-bye to him. Benetta was experiencing the same grief and loss as David. She was not rejecting her little brother, but she was unable to care for him, either. Meanwhile, Wayne loaded the boxes into his truck; then David and he headed for the bus station.

David's feelings of despair were unfathomable. He found himself on a Greyhound bus, headed for his sister Lameda's home in Liberty, Missouri, a suburb of Kansas City. He still searches for the right words to describe his emotions, unable to express the scope of the pain he faced that day: "Stunned. Hurt. Rejected. The whole thing kept coming back to me. Hurt on top of hurt. Rejection on top of that. Nobody wanted me. Nobody."

David had tried to argue his way into going to his sister Janice in Arkansas. But Bill, the brother with whom Janice lived, had suggested that David be put into an orphanage. He wanted no part in the care of a cripple, regardless of whether it was his brother. Bill, like many others in the family, had given up on David and wanted nothing further to do with him.

Liberty was two hundred miles from St. Charles, and during the ride, David began to dread the future.

"I remember thinking, *Here I am again in a big city, needing to meet new people. Living with new family members. Starting all over.*

"I didn't want to do it. I just wanted to die. I knew for the first time that I was a burden to people. Everybody had his or her own family to cling to, but I didn't have anybody to cling to. The pain was too great to bear.

"Looking back, I understand the reaction of my family. I was very difficult to handle, and they were just as desperate for a solution as I was. However, the pain was still very deep."

On Monday morning, Lameda took David to enroll at Liberty High School. He refused to get out of the car. She turned off the engine and said, "Let's go."

He balked. "I'm not going nowhere."

"Yes, you are."

"No! I don't want to. I don't want to go to school. I don't want to live with you. I want to die!"

"You have to live with me, because nobody else wants you!"

"No! I'm not going to live with you, and I'm not going to school, and you can't make me."

Lameda tried to force David out of the car. He wouldn't budge. "OK, Dave. You just wait until Dub gets home." Dub was her husband. Surely he could knock some sense into the stubborn teenager's head.

"Fine. He can beat me, but I'm still not going."

The debate raged on that evening. Lameda and Dub wanted to provide a home for David, but he was too lost in his obstinate grief to allow them to help him. As far as options were concerned, he was running out of them quickly.

Two days later, David was on the Greyhound bus again, bound for St. Charles. His sister Bonnie and her husband, Buddy, had agreed to allow him to live in their home.

It was his last hope. And David knew it.

"If I didn't make that work, you know, I might be put in an orphanage. Therefore, I told Bonnie and Buddy, 'I will go to school. I will get my act together.'

"I went to school, but I skipped school more than I went. Many times I faked being sick. My stomach bothered me.

"Some days the school would call Bonnie at work to come get me. She would leave work to find me in the nurse's office or the principal's office. She got fed up with that. She told me she was not going to come and get me anymore.

"I used to walk down to the bus stop, playing as if I were going to school, until Bonnie had left for work. Once she was gone, I walked back home and stayed home until it was time for the bus to come back. Then I walked down to meet the bus and acted as if I'd been at school all day."

David was getting "Ds" on his schoolwork, and Bonnie and Buddy had had enough. "I can't do anything with you. I'm going to ship you back to Liberty," she said. Bonnie found herself in the midst of an emotional breakdown, and after six months, David was back in Lameda's home.

It was June, and that meant he had the summer to readjust —again. School, of course, was the most difficult problem he faced. So David started to relax. Maybe it wouldn't be so tough in Liberty High School after all. He met a few neighbors, and they seemed friendly enough. He wasn't exactly happy, but his desperation was less intense.

Then came the first day of school in September 1969. David walked to the bus stop with his head down, dreading the ordeal of beginning again. Starting over, starting over— he was sick and tired of starting over. He was unable to imagine anything but difficulty as he shuffled toward the bus stop with the posture of a defeated, hopeless victim.

As he stood waiting for the bus, a girl from the neighborhood walked up and looked directly into his face. She laughed and in a mocking voice said, "Hey, retarded."

Any optimism David had gained during the summer burst like a bubble at the sound of her words. Thus began a new series of rejections in Liberty, Missouri. The outspoken girl was very popular and social, and because she called David retarded, everyone else chimed in with similar insults. The wound in David's heart was broken wide open and throbbed more painfully than ever.

When he looks back, David understands that in those days he had completely isolated himself from the people around him. He detached himself by keeping his eyes downcast. He answered questions in monosyllables and refused to initiate conversation. He rejected friendly overtures and, despite his intelligence, never earned a grade higher than a "C." David describes himself at fifteen years of age as a stereotypical victim, visibly withdrawn and lost in self-pity.

Today his posture is so different, his message so positive and uplifting that it seems unlikely that he is same individual.

Why do we get down in the dumps? Because we have our eyes on our circumstances. Let me tell you, get your eyes off your circumstances and put them on God. The Bible says, "In everything give thanks." Every time you get down in the dumps, it's because you have your eyes on your circumstances.

People come up to me and say, "Brother Dave, I feel sorry for you." Many people consider me a handicapped or disabled person because of C.P. They want to give sympathy to those who are afflicted physically.

If there is one word I despise in the English language, it is the word sympathy. That is because I realize how damaging it could have been in my own life.

A bunch of people think cerebral palsy is a handicap, but I have to beg their pardon. If I had my eyes on my circumstances, then it would become a handicap. It all depends on how you look at your situation. If we wallow in self-pity, then that becomes a handicap.

The people of God spend the majority of their time at a self-pity party even though they may be normal on the outside. Do you know what's wrong with self-pity parties? No one shows up but you!

We live down in the dumps because we're looking at our circumstances the wrong way. If I looked at my shaky body or my limitations, you'd better believe I would be down in the dumps. But the key is, view your situation not as a handicap but as a blessing of God or a tool He can use.

Thank God, I don't look at cerebral palsy. I look at what God does in my life, and it becomes a blessing. It's not a disability. I thank God for cerebral palsy.

Joy comes when you get the chip off your shoulder.
Joy comes when you get your feelings off your sleeve.
Joy comes when you quit feeling sorry for yourself.
I thank God for cerebral palsy!

How was the fifteen-year-old victim transformed into a victorious adult? What kind of recovery program did he choose? To which kind of therapy group did he belong? What was the process by which he chose to emerge step-by-step from his misery?

David Ring took the old-fashioned route to a changed life: he came to the cross of Christ. It took him a long, weary season to find his way. At the time, he didn't even mean to do it. His sister Lameda has been encouraging him for weeks to go to church, and he had steadfastly refused. Despite the fact that he occasionally listened, tears streaming down his face, to the gospel music he'd always loved, David and God had come to a stalemate. David could not accept His Creator's sovereign will regarding Leron's death.

Besides, going to church was a miserable experience anyway. As far as David was concerned, church was nothing but another uncomfortable social setting. He remembers vividly one particular evening.

"One night I went to church, just to get my sister off my back. She'd been on it long enough, and it was time she climbed off. That night I went in and I sat down. When the preacher got up to preach I said to myself, 'Man, I wish you would shut up!'

"The preacher shut up, but then the Lord Jesus spoke up. The Lord came to me, and He knocked at my broken heart. He said, 'David, I am standing at your heart, knocking, and if you only listen to Me and open the door I will come in, and I will have fellowship with you forever and forever.'

"Nobody ever told me about that.

"Nobody ever told me about a relationship with the King of kings and the Lord of lords. Nobody ever told me how the Lord Jesus could change my life. Nobody ever told me how He could become a friend to me.

"All my life I had religion stuffed down my throat, but nobody ever told me about a relationship with Jesus. That night I got up from my seat and came down to the altar. I got down on my knees and said, 'Lord Jesus, here I am. If You are really up there, if You really love me, come into my life. I'm a lonely crippled boy. I'm a nobody, but tonight I want to be a somebody.'

"Hallelujah! On April 17, 1970, I became a somebody because Jesus came into my life. I became a brand-new creature. God took away my old things and gave me new things. God took away my loneliness and gave me happiness."

Today David Ring *is* different, and he asks national audiences to take notice:

> Look at me, people. Look at me! I still walk with a limp. I still talk funny. But, "Oh, the joy that floods my soul, because Jesus touched me and made me whole."
>
> I'm not the same anymore. I don't want to die anymore. I want to live!

I don't have a daddy.
I don't have a momma.
I don't even have a healthy body.
But let me tell you what I do have. I have the grace of
God, and the Bible says that "God's grace is sufficient for
you and for me."

God's all-sufficient grace is the essence of David Ring's message to the world. David stands as an extreme example of what that grace can accomplish in one man.

He still struggles with discomfort and sometimes severe pain. He continues to face the abuse of the ignorant and the cruel, but he is unrelenting in his drive to let the world know that "bellyaching" is a waste of time. He declares, day after day, sermon after sermon, that when a person falls on his knees at the cross and is set free from his burden by the miraculous power of the resurrection, joy becomes his strength, hope becomes his companion, and enthusiasm becomes his attitude for living.

3

JUST
AS I AM

Sometimes when Christians discuss their transforming spiritual experiences, they use such phrases as "getting saved," "being filled with the Holy Spirit," "finding Jesus," or "coming to the cross." All of those are accurate expressions, but in the case of David Ring, the term "new birth" was especially fitting.

David's natural birth had been marked by tragedy and had resulted in the crippling condition that would be with him for the rest of his life. In his opinion, his condition had rendered him unacceptable to most people he met. In fact, after his mother's death, even the family members who genuinely loved him found him virtually impossible to be around. Although they were willing to accept his physical limitations, they found it difficult to cope with his negativism.

Being "born again" is a real spiritual event that happens through faith in Jesus Christ. No matter how healthy a person's body might be, Christians believe the Bible's diagnosis of humankind: all persons who come into this world are crippled; they are disabled spiritually by a sinful nature. They believe this nature acts out in unhealthy behaviors that are recognized as selfish and evil. In order to be born again, each person has to admit to God that he or she is sinful.

We must request forgiveness, based on the fact that God's perfect Son, Jesus Christ, has already paid the penalty for all human sin by dying on a Roman cross. Through faith in a resurrected Jesus, we are cleansed from our sinfulness. We are received by adoption into God's family of believers in Christ.

As soon as that spiritual decision is made, God's Spirit becomes resident within us. When God's Spirit enters into a person's life, that individual is said to be born again.

Jesus said, "Unless one is born of water and the Spirit, he cannot enter into the kingdom of God. . . . For God so loved the world, that He gave His only begotten Son, that whosoever believes in Him should not perish, but have everlasting life. For God sent not the Son into the world to judge the world, but that the world through him should be saved" (John 3:5, 16–17).

David Ring had heard about Jesus Christ all his life. He knew this gospel news. Furthermore, he had memorized all the familiar Bible verses that Sunday school children are taught. He had sung the songs, attended the services, and listened to countless sermons, many of which specifically addressed the matter of being born again.

It was all well and good for everybody else, but David had a great deal of trouble believing that the words "God so loved the world" applied to him. In his view, he was too ruined to be loved by anyone. He would have been more comfortable with the idea of a new physical birth—getting a better body—than a spiritual experience based on God's love for him.

He gladly would have exchanged his miserable life for a life of ease, comfort, and health. He hated his condition. He despised his limitations. He thoroughly disliked himself.

"I had a very poor self-image," David says. "I was down on everything and everybody. As I travel throughout the country today, I find more and more people who have the same problem with their self-image. This thing called *low self-esteem* can destroy an individual faster than anything else. I have seen it countless times. When we have low self-esteem, everything fails. It even keeps us from God.

When David thinks of low self-image, young people come to mind. "Poor self-esteem is probably the number one problem among [teenagers] today. That's why they explore alcohol, drugs, and sex. They have a void in their lives that only love can fill. They tried to fill it with anything and everything. Our youth are crying out, 'Somebody love me!' The only problem is, the love they're getting is a false love."

But poor self-esteem is not just a problem for teens, according to David. "Just because you aren't in puberty anymore doesn't mean you are exempt from this epidemic. I know people who are thirty, forty, fifty, and even sixty years old who don't love who they are. One reason young people have a hard time loving themselves is because the majority of the adults they live with have never really come to the reality of loving who they are either.

"We have to love who we are. If we don't learn that, we will have the tendency to be negative."

David likes to emphasize that esteem is not egotism. Esteem is respecting your person, egotism is glorifying yourself. David distinguishes the two this way: "I'm not talking about egotism. Egotism is being stuck on yourself or conceited. Being stuck on yourself is being preoccupied with caring for yourself and having a 'look what I've done' attitude.

"Egotism is making people think you have it all together, which you don't. It is a false advertisement of who you really are.

"Egotism is glorifying self, looks, popularity, things, or materials.

"Loving yourself, however, is seeing you as God sees you. Love is giving, and giving is loving. When we love ourselves, we want to give ourselves away to help someone else. We will be not a burden but a blessing.

"Loving yourself also provides a sense of confidence and security. You are secure in Him and in what you are doing in your daily life. You aren't afraid to attempt new things. You are positive.

"How do we love ourselves? We do it by seeing ourselves as God sees us. We are very special in God's eyes. When we love ourselves, we can love others. We begin seeing good in them. We stop finding fault with them.

"We will always feel defeated if we don't conquer this thing called low self-image. It will conquer or destroy us. I know. It nearly destroyed me. I told my family, 'Give up on me. I'm a no-good cripple. I will never do anything. I will never be anything. Just give up on me.'"

And almost everybody did; everybody except his sister Lameda. She encouraged him to go to school when he didn't want to go, when he feared he would be "the laughing stock of the student body." But "she encouraged me and wanted me to go."

"Lameda wanted me to go to church, too. I didn't want to go to church. I'd been to church all my life. I was the preacher's kid. I've been to Sunday school. I know the lingo. I even know John 3:16. But John 3:16, a verse everybody knows, didn't make sense to me."

And so David asked a series of questions—questions he repeats before large audiences as he speaks of his search for God's love:

If God loves me, why did God take away my daddy?
If God loves me, why did God take away my momma?
If God loves me, why did God give me a crippled body?
If God loves me, why is God picking on me?
If God loves me, why is God so angry with me?
If God loves me, why do bad things happen to God's people?
If God loves me, why is God breaking my heart?
I'm sure that most of you have asked God those same questions, haven't you?
If God loves me, why, why, why?

Though David did not have answers for those questions, he realized that if he was ever to have hope, it would be hope in Someone beyond himself. He finally said yes to Lameda's persistence by attending that April 17, 1970, service. That night, at the front of a simple Baptist sanctuary, David made a commitment to set aside his questions about God's motives and to accept God's offer of new life.

"I remember the day I quit asking why. Joy unspeakable came. When I asked, 'What?' instead of, 'Why?' I began to hear the Spirit of God."

"David, David."

"Yes, Lord."

"You're different."

"I know I am, God. Thanks for telling, me. I really appreciate that."

"Do you know why you are different?"

"No, Lord."

"Because I made you different."

"You did?"

"When you were in your momma's womb, I ordained you."

"You did?"

"You are very, very special."

"I am?"

"You are unique."

"I am?"

David finally realized that the why question could not help Him know God. As he explains:

> When I ask why, I don't hear. I don't see. But when I ask what, I begin to hear God speaking. And so shall it be with you. Don't ask why. Ask what. Because when you ask why, you will come up empty every time.
> Don't come up empty!

David Ring learned important lessons about acceptance the night he was born anew. First, he immediately recognized when he accepted Christ into his life that God had already accepted him—David Ring, the crippled boy—just the way he was.

"The night I made my commitment many emotions raced through my heart. Walking forward was traumatic. What will people think as I walk to the altar? Will they giggle or laugh? Will they accept or reject me? To be honest, the last was my worst fear. Nevertheless, I made the walk down the aisle. It was very difficult, both physically and emotionally.

"To my amazement, the response was absolutely overwhelming. The people of God gathered around and accepted me just as I was. Their love was truly an example of God's love. I think I know what the Bible means when it speaks of rejoicing in heaven among the angels when one sinner is converted. There was a lot of rejoicing that evening. It was an experience I will never forget."

David was able to accept the love of the people who surrounded him at the church altar, their arms wide open in love. In a different church on a different night years ago, Christians had welcomed Leron in her repentance. Now other good-hearted church folks reached out to her son in the same way.

It wasn't the first time they had tried to embrace David; their love had always been available to him. But until that night he had simply looked at his shoes and moved away. Now David Ring came to Christ just the way he was. His feelings of rejection were swept away by the overwhelming love of Christ and His people. David's life would never be the same.

Recalling his feelings of rejection to that point, he calls rejection "an empty word. When we feel rejected, nothing seems right. . . . Rejection is the worst feeling in the world. It is a lonely and miserable feeling. I'd rather be hungry than feel lonely and rejected. But many, many people feel rejected."

In churches and assemblies everywhere, David likes to contrast the rejection he had felt earlier with the new-found acceptance God gave him.

> *Before my decision for Christ, I felt rejected by God and everybody else. I felt rejected by God because of my handicap and the loss of Momma. I felt rejected by everyone else because they made fun of me.*
>
> *The opposite of rejection is acceptance. That is the salvation message—to go from rejection to acceptance. That is exactly what happened to me the night I gave my life to God. For the first time in my life, I felt accepted by Him. If He formed me in my mother's womb, He has surely accepted me. To know that He has accepted me is the greatest security I can have. When we are accepted by God, we begin to feel accepted by others. We have a common bond with each other. We begin to love others and reach out to them.*
>
> *When I realized that God had accepted me before I was born and that He had made me, I was able to accept myself. If He took the time to make me with cerebral palsy, I must be very special. And so are you.*
>
> *In fact, each of us is called the "temple of God" in 1 Corinthians 6:19. You and I are a dwelling place where He*

lives. If we are His dwelling place, you can be assured He has accepted us.

David's personal conversion took place when he waved a white flag and surrendered in his ongoing war with God. His perspective changed from bitter to sweet when he stopped raging about his limitations and instead submitted to the will of his Creator. His world was made new when he came to God, in accordance with the words of a beloved salvation hymn:

> Just as I am, without one plea
> But that thy blood was shed for me,
> And that Thou bidds't me come to thee,
> O Lamb of God, I come. I come!

Ever since his mother's death, the world around David Ring had said, "No, you can't." Once he relinquished his frustrations to the Lord, David learned to say, "I can do all things through Christ who strengthens me."

4

A NEW BEGINNING

Until the day of his spiritual rebirth, David Ring had had virtually no friends. He had had a few opportunities for companionship, but none of them had worked out.

For example, a boy named Tom at Liberty High School had suffered from polio as a small boy. One of his legs was shorter than the other, so he walked with a limp. He and David formed a tentative friendship, making small talk with each other. One night Tom invited David to go to a football game with him and a group of friends.

David agreed to go. But it didn't take him long to feel put off by the other boys' hard-drinking lifestyle and rebellious behavior. No matter how lonely or angry he might have been, that kind of conduct wasn't acceptable to David. He wanted nothing more to do with them.

Both at church and at school, Christian young people had made various attempts to talk to David, to reach out and care about him, but he had rejected their advances. At Liberty Manor Baptist Church, Pastor Don Wideman's son, also named David, had doggedly tried to befriend David Ring during vacation Bible school. Every time David turned around, there was the other David, trying to strike up a conversation. "I couldn't wait for him to stop talking and go away," David recalls, "so I just looked down, and answered, 'uh,' and, 'uh-uh,' to everything he said." David Wideman's perseverance ultimately paid off, however. David Ring eventually became a close friend of the Widemans.

In those painful, adolescent days, David assumed that people who reached out felt pity for him and that they were trying to do "the right thing" by talking to a cripple. Lonely as he was, he isolated himself whenever he could. He answered questions coldly, with monotone responses, and averted his eyes. Naturally, no matter how good an individual's intentions might have been, he or she eventually gave up on David.

His spiritual rebirth changed all that. Once his wall of self-protection tumbled down, David Ring found himself surrounded by new friends almost immediately. Other students were quick to discover that he was smart, courageous, and had a great sense of humor. His grades went from bad to good. It wasn't long after his walk down that Baptist church aisle that he found himself in the midst of an almost unbelievable situation.

The school term was nearly over. David was a junior. Several of his schoolmates wanted him to run for vice-president of the senior class. "I can't do that—a cheerleader is running for the same office," David protested. He might have been a new person in Christ, but how could he hope to beat a cheerleader in a high school class election?

His friends insisted. He thought they were crazy. It took them an entire month to convince him that he should try.

Nine short months after the incident at the bus stop when the popular girl had stared in his face and mocked, "Hey, retarded!" an unlikely scenario played itself out. Was it really the same David Ring who stood up in front of the entire Liberty High School student body—one thousand kids—and made his first public speech? Even he found it hard to believe.

Posters urging students to vote for him read "Ring is a girl's best friend. And David Ring will be your best friend if you vote for him." He spoke for five minutes and received a standing ovation. That day the election for senior class vice-president was held. Out of 252 votes, the pretty cheerleader received only 44. David Ring was elected vice-president by a landslide. His brief speech had helped him accomplish his mission. He hasn't stopped speaking publicly since.

"The one thing that amazes me to this very day is how drastic the change was in my life," David says. "The day after my encounter with the Lord I had a one hundred eighty-degree turn around.

"The very students who had made fun of me and ridiculed me started changing their attitude about me. The same student body that had ridiculed me later voted me to be the most popular boy in school. They also elected me to be Mr. School Spirit. That blows my mind because it was just weeks after they had seen me go to school with my head down like a whipped puppy. I had anything but spirit about me.

"Why the change? My physical appearance stayed the same. My walk and talk remained afflicted. But God changed my attitude toward everything.

"I began seeing things in a different way. Every day I met new friends just because I wanted to. I got involved in everything I could. I was manager of the football, basketball, and track teams. I still have fond memories of those days.

"It was then that I began to be able to laugh at myself. When I started laughing, it made my friends comfortable to be around me. They even laughed with me—not at me but with me.

After that, when someone began to mock David, his friends would defend him. His teacher of psychology once referred to David as "the boy who was born dead." David's friends saw how much that label hurt him, and one day after class a group of them confronted the teacher. They pointed out her insensitivity to his feelings. The teacher later came to David and apologized.

The turning point in David Ring's life came when he stopped questioning God's right to make him crippled. The moment he ceased to judge God's purposes he also ceased to see himself as a victim. Once David gave up his victim's stance, he was able to find permanent victory over his disabilities.

"It was amazing to see how changed my attitude was. I see all around me now that there are many people who need their attitude adjusted. We have to be willing, then God can change our thought life."

Meanwhile, as a former "victim," David now recognizes that many people choose to remain victims rather than deciding to be victors over their problems. They do that for a number of reasons.

For one thing, being a victim provides an identity: "I am a victim of cerebral palsy," or, "I am a victim of child abuse," or, "I am a victim of divorce." That identity immediately sets the individual apart as a unique person in his or her own eyes and in the eyes of others. Of course, as David came to understand, God had made him a unique person, anyway. He has proven that he doesn't need to play the victim's role in order to enjoy being himself, and he hopes to influence others the same way.

Victims seek sympathy. They cry out for help in the midst of their troubles. Sometimes they mistake sympathy, which they may get in response to their painful condition, for love. Often people are not enthusiastic about giving up their victim's role because they fear it will cut off the attention they receive from friends and loved ones. Sometimes victims are unwilling to assume the responsibilities required by "normalcy." They may think that because they are victims they don't have to work as hard, accomplish as much, or be as accountable as other individuals.

Some victims, genuinely wounded by the cruelty of assailants, schoolmates, relatives, or other individuals do not want to make emotional investments in others. They are socially reclusive and voluntarily isolate themselves in order to avoid the risks of getting hurt again.

At one time or another, David Ring has experienced all of the "benefits" of victimization. He remembers feeling that because he had a handicap, the world owed him something. He recalls the ever-present chip he had on his shoulder, the defensive posture he always chose.

David also had what was perhaps the most common trait of victims—the chronic quality of bitterness that seems to permeate their lives. When people question God's sovereignty and authority, David Ring knows from experience that they invite bitterness into their lives and hearts. His own battle came to a climax the night of his rebirth when he exchanged bitterness for gratitude.

He calls bitterness "the most hidden problem in our church today." Like a cancer consuming a body, "bitterness eats away at the soul." He detects a pattern to bitterness, a pattern of deception.

"People become bitter because they have not dealt with a particular circumstance in their own life head-on. No one likes confrontation, so we ignore our problems. Or we sweep them under the rug. Or we put them away in a deep, dark corner of our lives.

"Sad to say, some people don't even know they have it. If they were asked, "Are you bitter?" they would deny it and say, "Not me." In fact, one of the signs of bitterness is denial. But nobody can fake it for long. It will eventually surface. The lid will blow someday.

"Bitterness usually stems from the loss of someone or something. A spouse's death. A divorce. Loss of family members. Loss of a job. A broken relationship.

"After something bad happens, people get angry. They begin speaking evil about God or an individual, and little by little, bitterness creeps into their lives. Before long it engulfs them. They are enslaved to it. They are in bondage.

"Bitterness will choke out all the life and joy in us. It is the root of many of our problems. We try to change the fruits in our lives, but the fruit won't change until the root changes. Only the grace of God can overcome our bitterness.

"Paul admonishes us in Ephesians 4:31–32 to put away bitterness and forgive. When we forgive, we release others and ourselves. We're free at the moment of forgiveness, no strings attached.

"Don't blame. Don't be bitter. Forgive."

Today David Ring expresses his concern to crowds across America.

I'm amazed today, everywhere I go, every time I get up to speak. I'm amazed by how many hurting people I speak to.

I'm not talking about the worldly bunch. I'm talking about the family of God. I'm talking about the children of the family of God. I'm talking about the saints of God.

I'm talking about the people whose names are written in the Lamb's Book of Life. I'm talking about the people whose sin has been washed away by the blood of the Lamb.

Everywhere I go, people come up to me and say, "I'm hurting, I'm hurting!"

If I could open up your life, I would find some dark corner that nobody knows about. They don't know about the pain you're going through. I'm not talking about the body's pain. I'm talking about the pain that goes deeper than the body. I'm talking about the pain that nobody knows about but you and God.

*You might walk OK. You might talk OK. But down
deep in your heart you are saying, "I'm in pain."
We all hurt today, folks, but we are asking the wrong
questions. We are asking, "Why, why, why?" Don't ask
why, ask what! "What can I become because of the situation? How can I glorify God?"*

The spiritual change in David Ring's life, which took
place almost instantly on the night of his selling out to
Christ, was highly dramatic. At last he had accepted God's
decision to create him unique and exceptional. That change
in awareness is reflected in the thoughts and words of another
David, who wrote his Hebrew poetry centuries before.

> For you created my inmost being; you knit me together
> in my mother's womb.
> I praise you because I am fearfully and wonderfully made;
> your works are wonderful,
> I know that full well.
> My frame was not hidden from you
> when I was made in the secret place.
> When I was woven together in the depths of the earth,
> your eyes saw my unformed body.
> All the days ordained for me were written in your book
> before one of them came to be.
> How precious to me are your thoughts, O God!
> How vast is the sum of them! (Psalm 139:13-17 NIV*)

David Ring's second birth was indeed an exercise in the
acceptance of God's sovereignty, and the repercussions continue today. With new goals, new ideas, and new opportunities, he continues to forge ahead

He has accepted God's will, himself, and the love of
others, and the acceptance has affected his emotions—im-
parting to him joy, hope, enthusiasm, and peace of mind.

* *New International Version.*

Acceptance affected his intellectual response to his sur-roundings. It created a new pattern of reaction that said, "I'm open to new possibilities, and I'm going to make progress no matter how hard I have to try." He developed—and contin-ues to demonstrate—determination beyond measure.

Acceptance changed his physical responses as well. The more he struggled to succeed, the more his coordination im-proved. There are still limitations to the use of his small mo-tor skills. Shakiness remains in his hands, but unrelenting practice and determination made a difference both then and now.

Most of all, after his conversion, David accepted a call-ing on his life. He determined, before many days had passed, that he had something to say to the world. Something impor-tant. Something revolutionary. His message was radical and perhaps a little irritating. He wasn't sure how to get it across, but God gave him some startling ideas in the weeks and months to come.

Once he had found his own answer, he had one question to ask of others. It was burning inside him. He was only sev-enteen years old when he first sensed the call to preach, but he knew all too well how important it was. Today, he's still asking his question. It could sound insulting or condescend-ing if it came from a different man with a more illustrious background or a healthy body. It might seem flippant if it were said without a grin and a twinkle in his eye. But when David Ring makes his favorite inquiry, he never fails to get a thoughtful and even repentant response.

His listeners can plainly see that he is giving his all for Christ, courageously addressing thousands of onlookers— speech impediment, shaky hands, and all. "I have cerebral palsy," he says with a smile and not a hint of apology. "So what's your problem?"

5

A LESSON FROM MOSES

The congregation listened in astonishment to the young man's words. They knew who he was, and they were well aware that he had had a spiritual rebirth experience recently. But to sit and listen to him was quite another matter. No matter how difficult it may be for him to speak, David Ring has a way with words. He has a personal charisma that demands a listener's full attention.

This particular night, as he spoke of his struggle with God, his ultimate surrender, and his desire to be used by Him, not a sound could be heard in the sanctuary. When David finished telling his life's story, Ron Greene, the host evangelist who had invited him to speak, stepped to the pulpit and invited each member of the congregation to make a personal commitment to Christ.

People spilled into the aisles and made their way toward the altar. It was a sight David would not forget—two hundred people were present. All but four came forward, tearfully and humbly.

It was the first time David had given his testimony since his own trip down the aisle some months before. Now that he'd found the courage to stand up and speak in public (his first such opportunity since the high school election), he was gratified by the response. But he wasn't prepared for the private and personal encounter with His Maker that followed.

Speaking requires immense effort for David and takes a physical toll on him. He crawled into bed that night weary and drained, but his mind was racing. He was reliving the point in the service when the people had gotten out of their seats and moved forward to dedicate themselves to the Lord. It had been a wonderful moment, rewarding and encouraging. But the interval that followed his recollection brought forth an unexpected dialogue with the Almighty.

David equates it with another historic but similar conversation, one God had with Moses. As David explains, "He [Moses] was on the backside of the desert, tending a bunch of sheep when God interrupted his day with a burning bush. Moses was minding his own business. It was a normal day, and, all of a sudden, God called him by name from the bush. God seems to speak in the strangest places.

"As for me, I was lying in bed, minding my own business. And God said, 'David, I want you to preach.'

"I said, 'Who me? Lord, I can't preach. I talk funny. Lord, people can't understand me. Lord, I have cerebral palsy.'

"Can you imagine me telling God I have C.P.? I have a feeling He looked down and said, 'Really? You have to be kidding! Tell me something I don't know! David, I want you to preach.'

"'Lord, are You sure You want me to preach? Take a second look, and then call me.'

"He took a second look and, hallelujah, He still called me to preach. I got out of my bed, got my Bible, and turned to Philippians 4:13, which says, 'I can do all things through Him who strengthens me.'

"I'm not going to let a cerebral palsy body slow me down from bragging on Jesus."

In July 1971 God called David Ring to preach. At that time, David was scheduled to enroll at Southwest Missouri State College, where he'd intended to study to become a certified public accountant, following in the footsteps of his three older brothers.

Once he heard the call of God, however, David quickly changed schools. "If I'm going to be a preacher," he reasoned, "I don't want to go to a state school." William Jewell Baptist College in Liberty, Missouri, provided a ministerial scholarship of $500. David applied, was accepted, and enrolled there.

While a student at William Jewell, David deepened his friendship with Ron Greene, the same man who had first asked him to share his testimony.

"After that first opportunity, I went with Ron many places to share my story. I was with him every spare moment, and I learned about discipleship from him. He was a jolly man to be around and an encouragement to everyone. He always had a kind word to say. I wanted to learn everything I could from Ron.

"I remember one Sunday night when Ron and I finished a revival meeting in eastern Missouri. We had a four-hour drive back to Liberty. It was very cold, and the heater in Ron's car was out. We nearly froze to death. We put cardboard between the grill and the radiator, but we still froze.

"It took us seven or eight hours to get home because we stopped so often to get warm.

"Ron Greene was like a spiritual Paul to me, and I was like a little Timothy. He taught me many biblical principles that I still cling to today."

Ron owned a small bakery near the school. Sometimes David got up at four in the morning just to be near Ron as he made the doughnuts and other baked goods for the day.

Ron Greene believed in David Ring and in the call of God on his life. He urged David to get involved in a good Bible study, to read the Bible on his own, to memorize Scripture. Ron discipled his young friend until he was satisfied that David's daily walk with the Lord was in place.

With the encouragement of friends such as Ron Greene, David spoke every time he had the opportunity. When he had occasion to give an "invitation," allowing people to respond to his message, the results were always dramatic. Men, women, young adults, and children were inspired, encouraged, and challenged by his words—words that he persists in saying today, hundreds of times a year.

> *Look at me, people! I can't even say "Jesus" plain.*
> *What's your problem, healthy man?*
> *What's your problem, healthy woman?*
> *What's your problem, healthy teenager?*
> *What are you doing for the kingdom of God?*
> *I have cerebral palsy. What's your problem?*

Those words made a particularly powerful impact on Don Wideman, the pastor of Liberty Manor Baptist Church in Liberty, Missouri. Brother Don, as his church people called him, had watched David make his way down the aisle the night he received Christ into his life. He had witnessed firsthand the change in David's behavior.

It was Wideman's son David who had tried to befriend David Ring at vacation Bible school some years before. The night of his conversion, David joined Liberty Manor Baptist Church and was there every time the doors opened thereafter.

"The first time Brother Don invited me to his home," David recalls, "was for breakfast after the Easter sunrise service in 1971. From that day on, I was like a son to him and to his wife. They had four children of their own, and I seemed to fit into the family. Every Sunday I would go home with them for lunch, and after the evening service we would go back to their house for cheese and crackers. I still treasure those times around their kitchen table.

"The Widemans were a great encouragement to me. They laid a good foundation in my life. Their children were my best friends from my senior year in high school through college. I was one of the bunch.

"Don's mother lived with them. We called her Grandma Wideman—even I did. She was shaky because of a disease, and it became a joke every time we ate: which one of us will spill our drink first?"

Because of his special relationship there, David requested that Liberty Manor license him to preach. They were only willing to do so for one year at a time. He smiles at the recollection. "I guess they were afraid I would fail miserably and embarrass our church."

Although Don Wideman was extremely supportive of David as a "testimony giver," when David told him that he wanted to be a preacher, Wideman had some thought-provoking words for him.

"David, I don't mean to discourage you, but I would think twice about what you are doing."

"Why?"

"Well, David, you are very hard to understand, so many preachers won't invite you to speak because people can't understand you. I would think very hard about what you are going to do because you will never make it in other people's churches."

"Brother Don, I feel like God is calling me to preach."

"Are you sure?"

"Yes, I am."

"How do you know?"

"I just feel led to preach."

"I don't think so. I think you are hearing different people telling you different things."

"Like what?"

The pastor shook his head in frustration. "Look, David, I don't want you to get hurt. Being a preacher is a very high calling."

Don Wideman loved David Ring like a son. His heart ached at the thought of any rejection the young man might experience along the way. David accepted his words as they were given, lovingly and protectively. But David knew he had to pursue God's call.

David preached every other month throughout his freshman year of college and soon found himself on the college "revival team." That sent him to weekend Baptist revivals, where he gave his unique presentation of the Christian gospel in neighboring churches.

Once the local pastors in the surrounding Missouri communities learned that David Ring was willing to tell his story publicly, they invited him to share their pulpits for a few minutes during morning or evening services. They were delighted to have the earnest young man report his spiritual transformation to their congregations, and David loved doing it. Sometimes he was rewarded with ten or twenty dollars for his efforts. But for David, the money would never be as important as his mission—to preach the gospel.

God used two particular men in David Ring's life to help him fulfill that mission. Liberty Manor Baptist Church held a revival in October 1972. Clyde Chiles and Jim McNiel came to Liberty as the evangelistic team. They took an immediate interest in David. Together the three went everywhere, including school assemblies and eating out. With them David learned the "how to's" of evangelism. Clyde and Jim were professional, "yet they had a personal touch," David says.

The November after he met Jim, "Jim invited me to share Thanksgiving with his family. I'll never forget that day. As we were sitting around the table finishing our meal, Jim asked if I would share my testimony with his family. I did. It was a tender and teary moment. We all cried and rejoiced about what God had done in my life.

"After I got to know Chiles and McNiel, they began to invite me to tell my story on youth night in the various churches where they were holding revivals. I remember when I took my first bus ride to preach at one of their revivals. I was as excited as a little kid in a candy store. I had been on buses before, but then I had been defeated and lonely. This time I had a new message in my heart, a message of love and encouragement. What a difference!"

Jim and Clyde invited David to speak at youth night during a revival they were holding in Springfield, Missouri. David stayed in town during the weekend. He spoke at the Thursday night meeting, and on Friday night, January 7, 1973, God spoke to him—again—with another call to service.

Seated in the second or third row, David was listening to the revival message, which was on the subject of the Christian family. All at once he understood that God was "calling him into evangelism"—the Lord wanted him to challenge people to give their hearts and lives to God. That sudden awareness, or inner impression, was confirmed by a deep, warm peace.

At the invitation, David once more made his way to the front of the church, this time to publicly confess his obedience to God's call. When he confided his desire to be an evangelist to his friends, Jim and Clyde were delighted. They responded in a practical way, by including David in their itinerary whenever they could, even in out-of-state revivals.

Two months later David took his first plane ride. Clyde and Jim were holding a revival in Nashville, Tennessee, and had invited him to join them. David bought new clothing and joined the team. "God was amazing me every day with new opportunities," David says. "I really appreciated Clyde and Jim for seeing potential in me and for allowing God to use me."

The night God called David Ring to evangelism, another evangelist, Hubert Conway, was also present. He and his wife attended the service because they knew Clyde and Jim. Afterward, they all went out to eat. The Conways invited David to speak at their home church the following Sunday, just two days later. He did. From that time on, whenever Hubert was preaching close to Kansas City, David gave his testimony. Soon the relationship grew even deeper.

"As we approached the summer, Hubert asked me to travel full-time with him and his son, who did the singing. So I went with them everywhere all summer. When we weren't traveling, I stayed in their home in Mt. Vernon, Missouri. I had my own room. To this day they call it my room. I lived with them for two years.

"That family opened their heart and home to me. I felt accepted by them. They treated me as one of them. At Christmas, I had my own stocking. At Thanksgiving, I was there for dinner.

"I learned the faith principle from Hubert—how we need to walk by faith and not by sight. During one long night in the car trying to get home, he told me that God had led him to go to college with his wife and children. He had no money and only one jar of peanut butter in the whole house. They didn't know where the next meal was coming from. But God had always come through, whether by a check in the mail out of nowhere, or through an anonymous gift of food.

"I not only heard about it, but I saw Hubert live it. I learned what it meant to remain faithful to your calling in life. If we are faithful in the small things, then we will be faithful in the big things."

Those early days of preaching were not easy for David. Despite the encouragement of Chiles, McNiel, and Conway, hurts and disappointments still came David's way. Don Wideman had been right, in a way. There was no question that cerebral palsy was a major hindrance to a career in public speaking. No matter how spiritual his message was, David ran into obstacles based on prejudice, misunderstanding, and perhaps a lack of faith in "God's strength made perfect in weakness."

When he felt rejected, ignored, or ridiculed, David had to refocus his mind on what God had told him to do. He had to believe it was true, no matter how circumstances seemed to contradict his faith. He had to carry on and remember that the call on his life was not a figment of his imagination.

Today David preaches about God's call on the lives of all His people. Once again, he returns to the story of Moses in the Old Testament book of Exodus. David's message is direct:

> God said, "Go to Pharaoh and tell him: Let My people go."
>
> Moses said to God, "Who am I that I should go unto Pharaoh and bring forth your people out of Egypt? God, who am I?"
>
> Let me tell you, people, when you get saved, God will get specific later. God will always tell you what to do. When God tells you what to do, just do it. Don't say, "Who am I?" God knows who you are.
>
> The Bible says God knows you better than you know yourself. The Bible says God knows how many hairs are on top of your head.
>
> Many of you are giving God every puny excuse in the book. Shame on you. You say, "God, I can't. I can't. I can't." But the Bible says you can do all things.
>
> If God tells you to be a deacon, then "deac." If God tells you to be a preacher, preach. If God tells you to be a teacher, teach. If God tells you to be a singer, sing.
>
> "Brother Dave, I'm not qualified."
>
> That's right! Nobody qualified us but the Lord Jesus. It is not I preaching but Jesus in me.
>
> Do you know why we don't obey? Look at Moses. The Lord said to him, "What's that in your hand?"
>
> Moses said, "A stick."

God said, "Throw it down on the ground." Why did God say throw it down? Because it was in the way.

I can imagine Moses saying, "Well, Lord, I'm a pretty good shepherd, and all good shepherds need a good stick. This is my stick. You can go find Yourself any old stick. See the tree over there? There's a bunch of sticks on that tree."

God said, "Throw it down."

"Lord, you don't understand. This is my stick. You can count on me, but I'm keeping my stick."

The Lord said, "Throw it down."

"But, Lord—"

"Throw it down."

Finally Moses threw down the stick, and it became a snake. Moses ran from it. God said "Moses, Moses—"

If I were Moses that day, I'd have changed my name.

"Moses!"

"Yeah, what do you want?"

"Come on back, good buddy."

"What for?"

"Come on back."

"I'm back. So what do you want?"

"Pick up the snake."

"Sure, Lord. Look, you wanted the stick, and you got the stick. I don't want the stick anymore. I can go find my own stick. That tree over there, it has plenty of sticks."

"Pick it up, Moses."

"But, Lord—"

"Pick it up."

"OK, I'm going to pick it up. I'm going to pick it up by the neck."

"No, you're not. You're going to pick it up by the tail."

"Sure, Lord. Where have You been all your life? Number one, you don't pick up a snake. Number two, you sure don't pick it up by the tail. Lord, I don't want to. And, Lord, I'm not going to."

"Pick it up."

David Ring preaches and gives his testimony at church services
and youth meetings nationwide

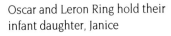

Oscar and Leron Ring hold their infant daughter, Janice

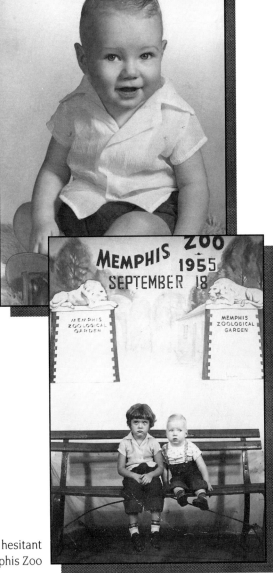

David at 18 months when his cerebral palsy was first diagnosed

MEMPHIS ZOO 1955 SEPTEMBER 18

MEMPHIS ZOOLOGICAL GARDEN

MEMPHIS ZOOLOGICAL GARDEN

Janice and David, two hesitant visitors to the Memphis Zoo

The high school years: David as a manager of the basketball team

David's senior picture

Receiving congratulations in 1971 after being licensed to preach

Three men vital in discipling David and leading him into evangelism: Evangelist Clyde Chiles

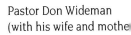

Pastor Don Wideman (with his wife and mother)

Evangelist Jim McNiel (shown with David)

David and Karen during their dating years

Below: David and Karen enjoy Thanksgiving Day with April Jane, then 18 months

No one was injured when the Rings' car hit a slick spot on a wet Florida road and rolled over three times. David escaped unharmed and preached four hours after the accident. (See Chapter 10.)

A family tradition: the Rings choose their Christmas tree in 1991

Below: The Rings today: Ashley and April (front); Nathan, David, Karen, and Amy Joy

Bible in hand, David Ring invites the audience to respond to his message and accept Christ as their Savior.

"But, Lord—"

"Moses, pick it up."

Moses *finally obeyed God. He reached down and grabbed the snake by the tail and picked it up. What did it become? It didn't become a stick, it became God's stick.*

Do you get the message? Moses threw down Moses' stick but picked up God's stick. But you say, "Brother Dave, what does that have to do with my life?"

Listen to me. Anything, anything, anything in your life keeping you from obeying God is your stick.

David Ring's stick was cerebral palsy. He was told on many occasions that he could not preach. He was reminded continually that he could not be an evangelist because of his speech impediment. He became discouraged and even wondered at times whether he'd heard the voice of God at all.

In physical terms, the discouraging words were true. It was difficult for David to speak. Going through the process of making himself understood was exhausting. Years of work would be required, including speech therapy, before he would speak with the skill and clarity he demonstrates today. But on a spiritual level, David Ring was capable of great things even then. God was blessing his efforts; the response to his preaching was evident. He had to keep trying.

David Ring, the hopeless, little crippled boy from Arkansas, was about to become a successful Southern Baptist evangelist. He had thrown down the handicap stick, and he says,

It became God's stick. From then on, everywhere Moses went with God's stick, it did a miracle.

I don't know what your stick is. You name it.

It might be your husband. It might be your wife. It might be your children. It might be your momma. It might be your daddy. It might be your boyfriend or your girlfriend.

It might be your school life. It might be your dating life.

It might be your home life.

It might be your job. It might be your money. It might be your church. It might be your preacher.

Anything that keeps you and me from obeying God is our stick. And God says, "Throw it down."

When you throw it down, God will change it into His stick. When you use God's stick, it's going to do a miracle.

A lady came up to me and said, "Brother Dave, pray for me."

I said, "OK. Why?"

She said, "Brother David, I do not have a stick in my life."

I said, "You don't?"

She said, "No, I do not have a stick in my life. I have a woodpile."

After that encounter, I thought maybe I should change my message from throwing down that stick to throwing down your woodpile.

What do you have in your hand? A stick? Or God's stick?

Not long ago David Ring received a letter from a man who met him in the early days of his ministry. It provides insights about his spiritual effectiveness, and it describes his personal impact on the lives of those who have heard him.

Dear David,

It has been many years since I have talked with or seen you, but recently I felt compelled to write. You probably don't even remember who I am—we only met two or three times. I was not a Christian when we met, however I was checking things out, so to speak.

You were working revivals with the evangelistic team of Hubert Conway and Gordon Watson. You never had the opportunity to know, but I did in time accept Christ. And I have thought of you many times since.

I never had the chance to say thank you, but you know how we get wrapped up in life, and lose sight of things. So let me say now, thanks for the many thoughts and insights that you so unselfishly shared many years ago. . . .

I had wondered where you were and what had happened to you. Then one day I was watching our local Christian TV station and guess who I saw—David Ring himself all the way from Thomas Road Baptist Church with Jerry Falwell.

As I listened to your testimony at Thomas Road, I felt very proud and happy for you that your faith has taken you so far with so many exciting opportunities to witness for our Lord. Your speech seems much clearer, and you seem to be getting around better also.

You know, David, God may not have given you a whole lot of talents, but you have used them to their maximum potential.

He may have given you many physical limitations, but you have maximized each and every talent that you do have.

You have led so many people to Jesus and have closened the walk of so many more, myself included.

You have been a blessing to so many, and have uplifted so many more.

You make an impact on people that is never forgotten.

You bless and enrich people's lives even though you haven't seen them in years.

David Ring has come a long way since his first speaking opportunities with Conway and Watson, Chiles and McNiel.

He has overcome extraordinary obstacles. He has achieved things no one would have believed possible. He has done all those things by responding to the call of God in his life and by trusting Him to provide the strength and success necessary to seeing that call of God fulfilled. Today he remains passionate in his encouragement of others to listen for the call of God:

When God calls someone, whether out of a bush or in bed, wherever it may be, He will always be specific. He told Moses, "Go tell Pharaoh to let My people go."

God always calls His children to service. The Bible says that the children of God are all members of one body. Each member has a task to do. If one member does not function properly, the body will become disabled or crippled.

If we don't do the work God has told us to do, we lose out on the blessing of serving. It takes everyone to complete the body. If we do our part, then the work of God will be accomplished.

Everyone can't be a preacher or a teacher, but we can be something. Many people say, "How can I know for sure what God wants me to do?" Or they say, "I'm not qualified to do that."

The bottom line is that we give God every excuse in the book. Moses did that by saying, "Who am I that I should go to Pharaoh?" At first he answered his call, saying, "Here I am, God." But the next thing you know, he's trying to renege on his commitment to the Lord by offering Him excuses. He even said, "I'm not an eloquent speaker."

It won't work, folks. Because God has equipped us to do His service. God said to Moses, "Hey, Moses, who made the mouth and tongue? I wasn't on lunch break when you were born."

In my own case, it was, "Who me? How can you use someone like me with a speech impediment?" I used the same excuse Moses did!

The dark shadow of discouragement haunted David's early years; even now he sometimes goes through times of struggle. But as God would have it, the issue of overcoming depression and discouragement was to become the very essence of his message. Who could better address such a common difficulty from such an uncommon vantage point?

Today, still obedient to his own "Lord, here am I" response, David Ring continues to share the lessons he learned. He is determined to encourage all of us to trust and obey, no matter how obscure the way, nor how impassable the path ahead may seem to be.

6

WALKING
ON WATER

What are God's people supposed to do when they feel discouraged? Sometimes men and women of God are convinced that they have heard God's direction for their lives, yet they find themselves faced with discouraging circumstances that seem to contradict His guidance. How should they respond?

David Ring felt called by God to preach, called to be a full-time evangelist. But obeying God's call wasn't easy. It meant overcoming physical handicaps. It meant going against the advice of well-meaning friends. It meant stepping out in faith when it wasn't safe to do so.

When God's people begin to live by faith and to have a personal friendship with Jesus, they eventually receive direction from Him. It is an inevitable part of the relationship.

The Word of God says, "And your ears will hear a word behind you, saying, 'This is the way, walk in it,' whenever you turn to the right or to the left" (Isaiah 30:21).

Of course, the direction we receive must be tested against God's Word; it must not conflict with the boundaries and principles of Scripture. But once we are confident that God has truly spoken, we are expected to obey. The Bible is full of stories about men and women, such as Abraham, who stepped out in faith, not knowing where they went.

We can expect opposition, unpleasant circumstances, criticism, threatening finances, unexpected illness, waves of discouragement. Those things inevitably block our obedience. When we encounter such obstacles, we soon find ourselves on our knees, crying out to God for assistance. Always gracious to hear and answer, He sends the support He knows we need most. He watches as we persevere, struggle, and wait on Him for help. He tests us in our obedience. He allows conflicts to strengthen our resolve, to carve His will deeper into our souls.

As David Ring struggled with discouragement, he searched God's Word for answers. He read the description of King David in 1 Samuel 30:6: "David was greatly distressed; for the people spake of stoning him, because the soul of all the people was grieved, every man for his sons and for his daughters: but David encouraged himself in the Lord his God" (KJV*).

Today David Ring explains how he finds relief from discouragement: "When we get discouraged, we keep searching to find out if anybody has good news out there. When we find it, we latch onto it and hang on tight. When we receive discouragement from people, we can always expect to receive encouragement from the Lord."

Having gained encouragement from God's people and God's Word during his own time of testing, David longs to share that encouragement with others. Often he sees unhappy, dejected faces in the congregations he addresses.

---

* King James Version.

There are many discouraged people in the church today. It might be because of problems with school, job, family, children, or whatever, but many of God's people seem to be carrying heavy burdens.

The church should be an exciting place to go. However, it seems to be the opposite. Some of the most boring people I know are in the church. They come to church, and they look dead. They look bored. You can find more people smiling down at the local morgue than you do in the church!

Why? Why do we look bored? Why do we look dead? Why don't we get anything out of church any more?

We come to church, and we look like we've been sucking on a dill pickle. At the same time we can go to a football game or a baseball game or some sports game, and we sit there and cheer for three hours and call that fun. But we come together at church, saying, 'Bless me if you can.'

Recently I went to a professional basketball game, and I was amazed by all the excitement in the air. I wondered, Why can't church be that way? How can fifteen thousand people get so excited about a basketball game or fifty thousand about a baseball game or eighty thousand about a football game, and at the same time you find churches filled with so many sad faces?

Why don't we get excited about the things of the Lord? . . . There's nothing wrong with basketball, baseball, or football, but they do not—will not—change your life. The Lord Jesus will and does change lives! Yet we get excited over the things of the earth.

None of the things of the earth has ever been quite as exciting to David Ring as standing in the pulpit and seeing men and women, boys and girls stream to the front of the sanctuary to give their lives to Jesus. After his conversion, that became his reason for living. That was evident fruit of God's call on his life. He knew he had to obey the Lord, and he also knew he had to rock the proverbial boat in order to do it. In fact, he compares the story of the storm of the Sea of Galilee and Christ's walking on the water to God's calling for our response and obedience:

> *In the fourth watch of the night, which is at 3:00 A.M., the boat was in the middle of the sea, and a storm came up.*
>
> *We can be sailing along in our own life, with everything going wonderfully, and all of a sudden, out of nowhere a storm comes up. You may be told that you've only got weeks to live. Or your loved one has just been killed. Or your teen-aged daughter is pregnant out of wedlock. Or your son is on drugs. Our your job has been terminated. Or your marriage is over.*
>
> *The old children's song says, "Merrily, merrily, merrily, merrily, life is but a dream." But you know as well as I do that life is not a dream. On the contrary, life is filled with many storms. We're either in one now, or we just came out of one, or we're headed into another.*
>
> *But I have good news. Whenever there's a storm, guess who always shows up? In the middle of the night, the disciples saw a man walking on the water. They did exactly what you or I might have done. They cried out in fear. They started screaming and shouting, saying, "It's a ghost!" They didn't recognize their own Master and Lord. Many times we can't see Jesus clearly because of the storm raging in our lives.*
>
> *Jesus immediately said, "Take courage. It is I; do not be afraid."*
>
> *Peter said, "Lord, if it is You, command me to come to You on the water."*
>
> *I love Peter! Peter opened his mouth just to change feet! Peter said, "Prove it. If that is you, Lord, let me come to you."*
>
> *Jesus said, "Come out of the boat."*
>
> *Wouldn't it have been easier for everybody if Jesus had climbed into the boat? But Jesus was on the water, and He wanted Peter to venture out. So Peter got out of the boat and walked on the water to get to Jesus.*

Why are we discouraged, defeated, or lonely? Why don't we have direction in our lives? Because we are not walking on the water with Jesus!

You say, "Brother Dave, I'm saved already." Being saved and walking with Jesus are two different things. There are many born-again children of God who are not walking with Jesus daily in their lives.

Isn't it about time you got out of the boat? I guarantee that walking with Jesus on the water is more exciting than sitting in the boat.

David Ring stepped out of the boat when he agreed that his future would involve public speaking. It had to be God's voice—who else would suggest such an impossibility? The obstacles he encountered verified the call to preach and to be a full-time evangelist.

Just as discouragement may come from many sources, so may encouragement. David says:

God speaks through many different avenues. Listen to Him. Obey Him. When opportunities come along, pursue them.

It takes faith to step out of the boat and walk on water. We are to walk by faith, not by sight. What is faith? Faith is the substance of things hoped for and the evidence of things not seen. Faith is a substance. Faith is knowing that the moment we get out of the boat, Jesus will always be there walking with us.

Though winds may come up and the waves may get bigger than life itself, Jesus is there. The storm may be raging, but Jesus is the peace that surpasses all storms. Faith is climbing out of the boat when people are telling us to stay in the boat. Faith is leaving the comfort zone. Faith is leaving all our security behind to walk on water with Jesus.

You've heard the expression "Don't go out on a limb." Well, faith is knowing there is fruit out on the limb!

> *The disciples probably discouraged Peter from getting out of the boat. I'm sure they said, "Hey, Peter, where are you going? You are going to do what? We love Jesus too, but don't go overboard. Sit down, Peter. You're rocking the boat."*
>
> *People in the church say, "Don't rock my boat, and I will like you." When somebody wants to get out of the boat, we all grab him and hang onto him and say, "Don't go! We love Jesus, too, but stay in the boat! Don't rock the boat! Sit down and take it easy. Don't be a fanatic!"*
>
> *I believe with all my heart that churches everywhere are hanging onto tradition, and we're hanging onto our heritage. But, people, walk with Jesus! Get out of the boat.*

When David Ring made his decision to get out of the boat, he took a lot of people with him. Many of them were pastors. In 1975, Don Wideman invited David to speak at the Missouri Pastors' Conference of the Missouri Baptist Convention in Cape Girardeau, Missouri. Although it was his first time to address that conference, David found himself in a key speaking position—11:30 A.M., Monday, just before lunch.

When he finished speaking, the pastors immediately inundated David with invitations to be a guest evangelist at their churches. Until that day David had carried his speaking schedule around in his brain. Now, for the first time in his life, he had to write everything down. There were too many dates to remember.

His message had been too revolutionary for those preachers to forget. Many of them had arrived at the convention weary, disheartened, and ready to quit. As he told his life story, he saw them weep. He heard them cry out, "Amen!" He watched them shout for joy. Away from their home churches and the critical eyes of their congregations, those Baptist pastors' spirits were lifted by David Ring's story.

Their hearts were saying, "If God can use David Ring, He can surely use me." They had heard a message of hope, and that message had renewed God's call on their lives.

David was deeply moved. All his life he'd fought discouragement. Now he found himself encouraging preachers who were feeling down. They were dealing with the pressures of church politics, with the financial stresses that never seemed to diminish, with the negative comments that greeted them after every Sunday service. Here was a man saying, "Hey, you think you've got problems? God will see you through them just the way He's taken care of me. Just keep your eyes on the Lord."

David echoes that message to men, women, and youth he meets across America. "Walking on water," requires a focus on God.

It is important, as we walk on water by faith, to keep our eyes on Jesus at all times. The moment we take our eyes off Him for any reason, we will go under. . . .

When I was twelve or thirteen, one of my older brothers allowed me to drive his John Deere tractor—with his assistance, of course. He was plowing the field, getting it ready to plant a crop of soybeans. He asked if I wanted to steer it.

I was thrilled. I was very careful as we made our way to the other end of the field. When we got there, he said, "Now look back."

When I looked behind me at what I had plowed, I saw the most crooked row in the world. My brother taught me a valuable lesson that day. He explained that to plow a straight row, you have to fix your eyes on an object at the other end of the field, like a tree or a telephone pole.

The same principle applies to walking on water. If we fix our eyes on Jesus, nothing will distract us. We won't get lost in the storm. Nothing will sink us.

As Peter began to look at his storm, he started gargling water. Then he cried, "Lord, save me!" Jesus reached out a hand and saved Peter.

You may be going under for the third time because of a marriage or a job or a wayward child or a relationship. What-

ever it may be, the Lord is on the water, ready to save you in
the midst of the your storm.

> Turn your eyes upon Jesus,
> Look full in His wonderful face;
> And the things of earth will grow strangely dim
> In the light of His glory and grace. *

David graduated from William Jewell Baptist College in
May 1976. Before graduation, he applied to attend seminary.
Many of his friends were going, and it seemed the thing for a
young preacher to do. Unfortunately, he encountered rejection once again.

The school declined David's application because of his
handicap. At first, old feelings washed over him in waves. He
felt left out, discarded, "not good enough." Gradually, however, he began to remind himself that people throw away broken things, but God doesn't. He uses broken things.

Summoning his courage, David prayed, "OK, Lord. The
door to seminary is closed. Please continue opening the doors
for evangelism." God answered his prayer.

One big door swung open in June 1978, when David was
invited to speak at the Southern Baptist Convention's Pastors' Conference in Atlanta, Georgia. It was held in the
World Congress Center and amounted to the biggest meeting
of Southern Baptists in the world. Bailey Smith, the president of the Pastors' Conference, had heard David speak in his
church the previous year and asked him to give his testimony
at the conference, knowing that the young, unknown speaker
would move the audience with his unique life story.

To his knowledge, David, at age twenty-four, was the
youngest preacher ever to address the general conference.
That night most of the audience had never heard his name

---

* Lines from "Turn Your Eyes Upon Jesus," words by Helen H. Lemmel. Copyright 1922 by Singspiration Music/ASCAP. All rights reserved. Used by permission of Benson Music Group, Inc.

before. When he stood at the podium, twenty-two thousand preachers and their wives were watching and listening. He looked around the auditorium, hoping to catch a friendly eye or familiar face, but all he could see were bright lights.

When he finished, however, those pastors were wondering how soon they could schedule him to speak in their churches. Once again, David had brought hope and vitality to God's burdened people.

The conference was an important milestone in David's ministry. The telephone began to ring off the hook, and he received more invitations to speak than he could possibly accept. Since 1973, David had been a Missouri evangelist. After Atlanta, he was recognized nationwide.

The impact of his message is reflected in the letters he receives from all fifty states and from all walks of life. The spelling and syntax aren't always perfect, and the handwriting can be difficult to read. But the message of renewed hope never fails to touch David's heart. One inmate in twenty-four-hour maximum security confinement wrote after seeing David's video in the prison chapel.

Recently my fellow Christian inmates were given the wonderful privilege of hearing your testimony on video tape, and we were really struck with the question, what is your excuse?

I found myself searching and I found none. I thank you for your testimony! . . .

We, as you got halfway through your testimony, had little tears in the corner of our eyes as we looked at each other including myself as I listen.

I was not ashamed of my tears and neither were any of the others. Your testimony has left an everlasting im-

---

---

pression on our minds. I found out that I was not as tough as I thought I was. You are much tougher than we are.

I also might mention that because of your testimony I am walking closer to the Lord than I have ever did.

"All my life I've struggled," David says, shaking his head in wonder. "It blows my mind to think that now I'm encouraging other people who are struggling." His messages have also brought letters from pastors, encouraged through tough ministry situations as were the pastors at the Baptist convention. But the most moving letters seem to come from others who are physically disabled. Many physically handicapped people feel an immediate identification with David, and he receives letters from many who are inspired by his message and example to trust God.

Dear David Ring:

My name is Debra. I was born with cerebral palsy. I am 19 years old and I come from a family of five, two brothers and tow sisters. I am the baby and proud of it!

As I deal with my problems I always remind myself things could be so much worse and if I continue to try hard enough I will become better. I often think about your sermon "Why Do Bad Things Happen to Good People?" To begin with I had a hard time dealing with it all, but now I just take one day at a time with the Lord, and smile through it all.

I would appreciate it if you would keep me and my family in your prayers. I will continue to keep you and your beautiful family in my prayers as well as your ministry to others. Your have touched our hearts.

One man had suffered a sudden loss of his voice. Thinking he had simply a cold or laryngitis, he tried to wait it out. But when he did not recover, he went to his doctor. He went to several doctors, but each one told him that he would never speak again. Test after test turned up negative. No one could explain why he had lost his voice. Even exploratory surgery left the doctors dumbfounded. In a letter to David Ring he explained what happened next.

Finally during a church service, I asked the Lord if he would restore my voice. If he would, I would do whatever he wanted me to do with my life. But I just sat there during the invitation.

Not long afterwards, you preached in Toccoa, Georgia. . . . You were preaching on "Why bad things happen to God's people." You made a statement that I still remember today, "When we are weak, we are strong."

After you got through with your message I had tears running down my face because I knew if I didn't go down during the invitation I would never get another chance.

I went down that night and dedicated my life to full time Christian ministries doing whatever the Lord wanted me to do.

You see something wonderful happened that night. I got my voice back fully and completely, not a scratch in it.

I am a living miracle that God does hear and answer prayers because I had a lot of wonderful brothers and sisters praying for me that whole time.

The doctors were amazed that I got my voice back when I went back to them after I returned home. The very next Sunday I gave my testimony and sang "How Great Thou Art." Today I am still singing and praising God for giving my voice back.

In getting out of the boat and walking on the water, David Ring has brought many others into faith with him. He continues to challenge his listeners toward a life of faith, not sight.

Many years ago, he heard the voice of God calling him to step out. Despite discouragement and difficult circumstances, he persevered. Like King David, he "encouraged himself in the Lord his God" (1 Samuel 30:6 KJV). He has been more successful in his ministry than anyone would have dared predict, and he continues to encourage all of us.

"Let me ask you something," he says. "Think about it. Are you still in the boat?"

7

A WOMAN NAMED KAREN

Many times in David Ring's early years he was told, "Not you—you can't do that." Some people limited him because they were unable to grasp his capabilities. Others tried to protect him from disappointment, not wanting to see him try and fail. And there were those who didn't want to struggle through the process with him; they weren't willing to invest their patience in his dreams. So many people, particularly those in his own family, believed that he could not and should not marry.

The longing for a soulmate and lifetime companion had always been deeply hidden in David's heart. He hadn't spent much time with girls in high school or college. His natural shyness made it difficult for him to ask for dates. Because he'd been turned down a few times, his fear of rejection usually overwhelmed his willingness to try.

One by one, as his friends began to marry, he silently pondered the question, "Will it ever happen to me?" He visited his friends in their new homes, sharing their joy but privately wishing that he, too, could go home to a bride of his own. After he spent time with his newlywed friends, his apartment seemed lonelier and emptier than ever before.

David kept his yearnings about marriage to himself. Even though he was a young man with vision, reasonably handsome, and a bachelor, no one seemed to give any regard to David's potential for finding a mate. Even his own expectations were negligible as he drove toward St. Charles, Missouri, in May of 1979.

He had left for St. Charles as late as possible that day, because, frankly, it was his least favorite city on the face of the earth. David had suffered his most unforgettable humiliations at St. Charles High School during the months he'd spent at Benetta's home. Worse than that, he had heard the news about his mother's death there. It was in St. Charles that his ultimate abandonment had occurred when his mother had forsaken him by dying.

As he drove into town, his thoughts were dark. He found himself reliving those terrible days. He asked himself a question that, by then, was an unusual one for him: *Will the church in St. Charles reject me?* No matter how different his attitude might be now, he couldn't imagine anything but suffering happening to him in the city of St. Charles, Missouri, even at a church that had invited him to lead a week of revival meetings. Only his sense of responsibility kept him heading in the right direction, along with a quiet, inner voice that said, "Show them how much you've changed."

In retrospect, it seemed a touch of divine grace and mercy when David realized that St. Charles First Baptist Church was located on the same street as St. Charles High School. The name of the street was Kingshighway.

Wherever he spoke in those days, David always mentioned his single status. Everybody laughed heartily when, in various church pulpits, he scanned the audience slowly and said carefully, "I'm twenty-five, I'm single, I'm good-looking —and I'm looking." Hardly anyone took him seriously when he added, "I'm taking applications at the end of the service."

But that Sunday, one woman nudged her daughter and said, "Get your application in." The woman may have been kidding, but her pretty, eighteen-year-old daughter, Karen, wasn't.

"What happened between us was instantaneous," Karen says now. The minute she saw David she was drawn to him. Until she met David, Karen had dated a completely different kind of young man. Fine-boned, delicate, and feminine, she had attracted macho athletes. And she had been very hurt.

David enjoys remembering that first encounter.

"The Sunday night I met Karen, it all began with a casual greeting at the door as I was leaving the church. I remember thinking, *She is a pretty girl.*

"On Tuesday night, two days later, we talked at the tape table.

"The next night, I said to her, 'I would like to get to know you better.' That was my way of asking her out. Of course, I was afraid of rejection, afraid she would not respond. To my astonishment she replied, "I would like to get to know you better too."

"So we went out for a Coke®. In fact, we went out three nights that week.

"On Friday night, we went to Pizza Hut after the service. We went with another couple. When I took Karen home, neither of us knew if we would see each other again. But the next morning I went by her house to tell her good-bye before I drove to my next engagement.

"I had about seven hours to drive. All the way there, I tried to think of an excuse to call her.

"When I arrived at the motel, I found a $10 bill in a love offering envelope that she had placed in my car. There was my excuse—I had to call her to say thank you.

"The following Monday, I just had to take the long way home to Kansas City. It was four hours out of the way, but it happened to go through St. Charles. If I was going through St. Charles, I might as well stop and see Karen.

"We ended up spending three wonderful days together."

As soon as Karen got to know David, she felt accepted by him. She knew, considering his background and unique circumstances, that he could be trusted with her love. He had depth and spiritual maturity.

As far as David was concerned, Karen was a miracle.

"I couldn't believe we were dating. Jim McNiel led the singing at the revival where Karen and I met. I remember telling him over and over again, 'She is so beautiful. She is just gorgeous!'

"Karen was the kind of girl I only dreamed about going out with, much less falling in love with. My low self-esteem kept saying, 'How could someone like me be dating a girl like Karen?'"

Karen began her own process of "walking by faith" when she met David and fell in love with him. She recalls her feelings.

"I remember when I first saw him. Our church was anticipating a great, week-long revival with an evangelistic team. I was anxious as always to hear what the evangelist had to say. One of my friends had told me, "He's good. I've heard him before." So I listened.

"At first I thought, *Is this a joke?* I knew how preachers loved to joke.

"But this was no joke. David was real, and it was only moments before I, along with everyone else, was captivated by his story. *An amazing man*, I thought, *with an amazing story.*

"I walked down the aisle that morning, sincere in my heart before the Lord, asking God to use me more fully and completely.

"Later, I couldn't stop thinking about David. I invited a young man whom I had dated to go along with me Sunday evening. That's when I got my first glimpse up close. Yes, he was my kind of man. Blond, of course. Blue eyes that won my heart. But there was more. His story intrigued me.

"*What is behind the man in the pulpit?* I wondered. I longed to really know him. My mind was flooded with questions. I wanted to ask how he saw me too. Finally we shared a moment of conversation. "Hello, nice to see you."

"That was all I needed. I was now determined to get to know him. Tuesday night I decided to make the plunge at the tape table. I really was interested in his tapes, and besides, it would give me an opportunity to talk to him a little, which I did.

"Wednesday evening, I think I discovered that I needed another tape. So back I went. This time our conversation was really interesting. We discovered that he had attended my high school when all his years of turmoil were just beginning. He told me how he hated that school and really did not like St. Charles because he had so many bad memories there. Nonetheless, he said he'd like to get to know me better. I said the same, and off we went for our first Coke."

David proposed marriage to Karen just two weeks after they met. Confident in her decision, she said yes. Several years earlier, she had felt the call of God to marry a man in ministry. As far as she was concerned, David was the man. She recalls:

"We drive by a house and see the outside first. But the inside is where people live. I longed to know the man inside, and he was the man I fell in love with. He was a man who was caring, compassionate, and giving of himself and all that he had.

"David was a man who loved people and loved his God. He was stable, unshakeable, and unmovable in his faith. He had direction in his life. He was sure of his calling and unwavering in his convictions. Who wouldn't want a man like this?"

At first, concerned friends asked Karen to be sure that she was making the right decision. Would David be able to support her for the rest of his life? Was he capable of being a "normal" husband? Could they have children? The last question was the only one that concerned Karen's family—they knew how dearly she longed to be a mother. Otherwise, they loved David immediately and were delighted with the engagement.

The reaction from David's family was altogether different. Every one of them was adamantly opposed to the idea of David being a husband. Lameda, the sister David had lived with the longest, was chosen as the spokesperson for the family and tried to convince David that he should not get married. She tried to stop the wedding on several occasions. It wasn't Karen that the Ring family didn't like. It could have been anyone—any woman who wanted to marry their brother David. They tried everything to sabotage the relationship. Their motivation was fear—they were deeply and sincerely afraid that David would be hurt. Four days before the wedding, Lameda invested two more hours, begging David not to go through with the ceremony.

In actual fact, David nearly did cancel the wedding—not because of his family's disapproval but because of his own deep wounds. He knew he loved Karen. In fact, as much as he could, David was giving Karen all his love, all of himself. But in the back of his mind, he knew that he'd lost nearly everyone he'd ever loved.

David and Karen both laugh when she explains, "It took two weeks for him to propose to me and two and a half years for me to talk him into getting married." David Ring was about to develop a terminal case of bridegroom's cold feet.

His fears were due to the many personal rejections he suffered through the years.

"The two years of our courtship brought many struggles," David says. "At the beginning of our relationship, I feared getting a 'Dear John' letter, saying, 'Hit the road, I've found another guy.' The fear was justified because not long before meeting Karen, I had received a letter like that from a girl I'd been dating. It had left me desperately hurt.

"After I started falling in love with Karen more and more, my question was, could I love her with my whole self? After all, the lady I loved with all my heart had abandoned me in death. My momma had betrayed my love by leaving me. I wanted to express my love outwardly, but I was afraid.

"Our dating life was a lot of fun. We got to know each other very closely, very well. Yet there was a part of me that was constantly pulling back. That caused a lot of ups and downs. Karen desperately tried to figure out this man she was in love with.

"I felt that maybe she would get fed up with our ups and downs, with my changing our wedding plans, and that she would call everything off. In a way, that would have relieved me of the fears that I just couldn't seem to shake.

"That is exactly what happened, but not the way I thought. The chains of bondage that enslaved me had to be broken before I could ever truly love Karen the way Christ had intended love to be."

All too quickly the wedding date approached. When it came to the point of actually "tying the knot," David's ambivalence rose up and refused to allow him to go forward.

During their engagement, David phoned Karen every day and every night. Two months before the wedding, he placed his usual telephone call on a Sunday afternoon. By then all the wedding plans had been made. The invitations were ready to be sent. He knew that if he wanted to back out, now would be the time. David didn't really mean to call everything off permanently; he was just looking for another postponement. He had already procrastinated three times before, and it was getting easier each time.

Karen, a sensitive and intuitive person, had felt David's increasing reticence in the past few weeks. She had been bracing herself for another disappointment. In fact, when he suggested postponing the wedding, she was ready. She said, "You're not going to do me that way again. It's now or never."

"Fine," David answered abruptly. "Then it's never!"

Karen had weathered the other three setbacks and was more or less resigned to another. But at the same time, she'd treasured two and a half years of hopes and dreams, and David seemed to have given little thought to her pain. *How could he ignore my investment of time, dedication, and emotion in our relationship?* she asked herself. Yet with his one negative answer, he seemed to be doing that.

When David said "never," Karen really believed that the courtship was over. She was downstairs in her room, and her family was upstairs. She didn't say a word to anyone, choosing to be alone with her tears. She had only herself to blame—everyone had cautioned her. She wept bitterly.

Feeling dazed, struck by the suddenness of the loss, David hung up the phone. Immediately he got down on his knees. He prayed a desperate prayer:

"God, I need to know now. Not tomorrow, not tonight, not a week from tomorrow. I need to know now if Karen is the one for me. If she is the one You have put in my life, give me peace."

"It was a battle," David admits. "I was fighting not against Karen but against my own will. I was desperate in my spirit to settle the issue once and for all. It is not until we come to the point of total helplessness in our lives that God is able to break through our stubborn hearts. The moment we completely surrender our emotions and will to Him, sweet and wonderful peace comes. That is just what happened to me in Nashville that July Sunday afternoon.

"The peace of God came over me. It was so immediate and complete that it was as if I had been born again. I called Karen. She was crying. Thirty minutes with God, and I died to my fear."

Today they both realize that David had not fully released his mother's death until that time. He had clung to her memory and still mourned her passing. On his knees, about to lose the wife God had prepared for him, he gave up his lifelong attachment to his mother. Only then was he able to welcome Karen into his life with open arms.

"Even though I was already God's child, I had been having a battle within myself," David explains. "Many people in the family of God have a constant struggle in their lives because they cannot be free to be themselves. They are not free to express their true feelings to someone else. They carry excess baggage—burdens from the past. Until we release all of that to our heavenly Father, we will not be able to experience the joy of real living. If the Son shall make you free, you shall be free indeed."

The next day, Monday, David left for Oklahoma to speak at a youth camp. Upon arriving the first thing he wanted to do was talk about the engagement with the youth minister. "That was unusual for me," David says, "because in the past two years I had kept my so-called engagement quiet. Now things were different.

"We were now able to bond together in our spirits. We both began to work toward the same goals. Karen had made most of the wedding plans by herself, and when she consulted me I had given her only halfhearted comments. Now I was ready to give my whole self to our plans for the future."

The wedding was beautiful. It took place in St. Charles, Missouri, at Karen's home church. Surrounded by friends and family, the couple exchanged their vows. David recalls the scene with the passion of a newlywed once more:

"There were many tears of joy, but none like my own tears as I watched my beautiful bride walking down the aisle that evening. The glow on her face revealed the love that was in her heart. My eyes met with hers, and it was as if we were the only ones there at that moment. I was fully aware not only of the miracle of God's giving me Karen but of the work He had done in my life to bring me to this day. It was truly the work of our Lord. It seemed most appropriate when Jim McNiel, my best man, powerfully sang the words "To God be the glory, great things He has done."

Before a year had passed, David's family finally accepted him as a husband and approved of the wife he had chosen. And despite David's use of the word *never* that Sunday afternoon a couple months before the wedding, Karen believed in her husband's love.

"Even through all our growing pains and hurtful feelings, even through my own lack of understanding of his difficulties, I never doubted David's love for me. I never questioned that he was God's man for my life.

"Had those doubts come, perhaps I could not have withstood the storms. But God strengthened me and held me up to prepare the way for the future. It is comforting to know that God causes all things to work together for good to those who love Him and are called according to His purpose.

David had told Karen in one of their first conversations, "I hate St. Charles. I wouldn't ever want to live here again." But God delights in replacing life's bitter waters with sweetness. For David Ring, in his bride's Missouri hometown, God exchanged present beauty for ashes. Kingshighway led to the future God had always planned for His son David Ring.

8

A WIFE TAKES INVENTORY

The Rings settled in St. Charles, and in their first apartment they shared deep, tender happiness. Karen traveled with David most of the time that first year. Before long, God provided a way for them to purchase their first home. They knew that the foundation for their future was being laid by their heavenly Father.

"Fond memories flood my mind," David recalls, "of evening walks with Karen around our neighborhood. We would share our joys, our concerns, our intimate goals, and our hopes for the future. In order to have a strong marriage I believe it is important to find a time in the day when you can get alone together and put everything else aside to focus on each other.

"That's what we did then, and that's what we're still doing today."

The spiritual dimension of David and Karen's marriage brought her to an uncomfortable awareness during those first months. Everything seemed nearly perfect, yet Karen had an unsettled feeling about her own spiritual state. She would soon come upon a surprising discovery.

"Everything seemed wonderful—almost perfect—on the outside of my life," Karen recalls. "I was happily married to a man I deeply loved, had a brand new home and a precious new baby. Yet, in the midst of all that, there remained a gnawing emptiness within me that I just couldn't seem to fill.

"I remember a long, endless drive to Memphis, Tennessee. We were to begin another revival. On the way there I told David that I felt I needed something more in my life and I had decided to go back to school. After all, I only lacked thirty hours to receive my teaching degree, so it seemed like a reasonable decision. But even as my mouth was saying one think, my heart was speaking another.

"Traveling had broadened my own scope of God's family and the church," Karen continues. "Being around God's people, I realized that there was something in their lives that I was missing. Even David's life was a constant reminder to me of the void in my own heart.

"Throughout our first year of marriage, little by little, God began to lift the veil from my heart. For the first time, I realized my own personal sinful state and my need for Christ. An intense battle began within me.

"Ever since I had been a young teenager, I had longed for God, for His will to be done in my life. Growing up in the church, I was familiar with the gospel. I had done all the things I was supposed to do.

"Yet now I knew that it would not be enough to get me into heaven. It would not be enough to satisfy the gnawing emptiness in my soul.

"After a long inner battle against my pride and will, I surrendered to the greatest call a person can have in life—the call to salvation."

Karen had grown up in the Baptist church. She had taught Sunday school, attended church events, and even made personal commitments about her life. But now she knew her personal salvation had never been settled. So after one year of marriage, an unexpected event took place. David recounts the incident:

"I got back to the hotel about midnight. My wife was getting ready for bed, and she was crying. I mean crying hard. Being married only fifteen months, I asked the obvious question, 'What did I do now?'

"She said, 'You didn't do anything.'

"I said, 'Who called you? Did your Mom call? Did somebody die? Why are you crying?'

"I'll never forget the look on Karen's face. She looked at me, and she said, 'Dave, I'm lost. I've never been saved. I want God to save me.'

'Say what?'

'I want God to save me.'

David relates his reaction to his wife's astounding request. "I was stunned and almost speechless. I had always found it easy to share the plan of salvation because of the work that Jesus did in my own life. But this was altogether a different matter. This was my wife.

"I couldn't help but immediately think of the kind of person Karen was and her strong testimony. She had told me how she joined the chuch at the age of thirteen. How she was baptized. How she sang in the choir. How she went to a Baptist college. She won a bunch of people to Jesus. She even fell in love with a preacher and married him. Now she was a preacher's wife. What did she mean, she was lost?

"I groped for words and prayed for discernment. Karen explained how, only hours earlier, while at the church altar, she had battled intensely with God's call. She hadn't yielded for fear it would affect our ministry. It was quite evident that the Holy Spirit was at work. For added spiritual guidance and emotional support, I called the pastor of the church where our revival was being held.

"A short while later, at 1:05 a.m., my wife and I and the dear pastor of that church were down on our knees before our Lord. Karen so sweetly held up the white flag of surrender and cried out, 'O God, I'm calling on the name of the Lord Jesus. Save me now.'

"Praise God, on November 21, 1982, my wife was saved," David says.

"The following evening," David continues, "Karen shared her experiences with the church, and I had the glorious privilege of baptizing my wife. This was not only a new beginning for her, but for both of us. We were embarking on a new pilgrimage together."

Today Karen sums up that extraodinary experience. "The moment I finally surrendered myself to the Lord, I felt His peace and had full confidence I was His child. But it wasn't until I walked with Him in the weeks annd months ahead that I witnessed the true fruits of salvation. I felt like the thirsty woman drinking from the well that never ran dry. My desire for intimate fellowship with my Creator drove me to seek His Word. All the Scriptures I had read before, even those I had memorized, were like a fresh morning dew for me. Blessed are they that hunger and thirst after righteousness, for they shall be filled!

"My life was like a puzzle. I had put all the pieces so beautifully together myself, but that last piece was missing. As I so desperately tried to find the right piece, nothing fit. It was only when I was willing to give up the struggle that Christ could fit His life in mine. He was the missing piece. And now I am complete."

Both David and Karen Ring believe that God chose them to be married to each other. They believe that He prepared them, before the foundation of the earth, to be one in Him. The tenderness between them is almost tangible. It radiates from their eyes and colors their words. Once there was a spiritual separation, though neither realized it fully until that night of great tears by Karen, followed by repentance and restoration. Rejoicing greatly, David and Karen knew heaven now awaited them both.

Their life together still is marked by physical separation because of David's frequent travels. But David smiles as he says, "Even when Karen's not here, Karen's here." He remains aware of his wife's loving presence, no matter where he goes.

In addition to being married to the man of her dreams and God's choosing, Karen enjoys her role as mother of their children—the children no one believed they could have. Her faith has been rewarded; her blessings were worth the wait.

Because he discusses aspects of his own private journey when he speaks, many people write to David about their own personal problems. Because he is successfully married, David sometimes hears about marital difficulties that his listeners encounter. One neurosurgeon was facing divorce after nineteen years of marriage. He had worked hard to support his wife and family, but somehow things did not work out as he expected.

> I want to tell you how much your testimony meant to me. . . . The reason I write to you is to ask for you to please pray for me and my family. We are separated and things look very grim. . . .
>
> May I say that I have given my life to Jesus and asked him to give me strength and guidance and to touch the heart of my wife. Please pray that she too can see that it is only with the love of our Lord that we can ever hope to survive as a family. . . . .
>
> I thank you for reading this letter and for lifting up our problem to our Lord Jesus in your prayer. God bless you and your family, brother.

A woman, struggling with grammar and spelling, spoke lightheartedly of her marital struggles:

I'm writting you this letter on Sunday morning, November 29. When I got up this morning preparing to go to church, my husband would not get up to get ready. I continued to fuss at him til 8:10 a.m. to please get up. I finally decided it was to late so I sat down with a cup of coffee and turned on the t.v. to see if there was a service on I could watch. So full of anger cause we couldn't go to church. When I came across you preaching, I sat and listened and the more I listened the more I realized there was a reason my husband didn't get up.

David your message opened my heart and made me realize with all the financial stress and problems we are really facing, nothing is impossible thru the Grace of God to conquer.

Thank God for my lazy husband this morning and praise God for you, David. You don't know how much your mesage has touched my heart and made me see we will make it thru the IRS and all the old things satan continues to thru back at us.

To see Karen and David Ring together is to see an example of God's paradigm for marriage. They aren't without their own struggles and sorrows; in fact, they probably have more than their share because of their unusual circumstances. But the love that binds them together is more than an emotional feeling or a romantic impulse. David eloquently says, "Until I met Karen, for more than ten years God had been my constant companion and friend. It seems when we get married that God, our unseen friend, becomes revealed in someone else. My dream of having someone to hold, love, touch, and even share my innermost thoughts was now fulfilled. It was truly a gift and miracle of God."

David and Karen found each other through the guidance of God. They chose each other because they shared a commitment to God's work. They stayed together, even in their darkest hour of nearly parting, through God's gracious answer to their prayers. Today they epitomize the words of Isaiah 40:31: "Those who wait for the Lord will gain new strength; they will mount up with wings like eagles, they will run and not get tired, they will walk and not become weary."

9

A DADDY'S LOVE

Dear David,

My wife and I appreciate your video ministry. The "bellyache" tape is our favorite. We saw it for the first time soon after the death of our nine-year-old son in 1990. I believe God has intended for us to be a witness to how we should accept and even welcome the crosses life has for us to bear. The tape really helped.

God has also been willing to provide additional blessings. Eight weeks ago we were blessed with a precious new baby boy.

By the way, I am an ob-gyn M.D. and I share your approach to babies that are less than perfect in the world's eyes with many couples. . . . Thank you for the witness and the blessing you have been to us.

uch letters pour into David Ring's office day after day, week after week. Some are from healthy men and women with personal problems that have been put into perspective by one of David's messages. Others are from handicapped people who have been challenged by his call to excellence. Many of the letters are from people who have struggled with loss or disability in their own children. Virtually all of them agree wholeheartedly with David's point of view about "normal" children.

David's approach to "babies that are less than perfect in the world's eyes" encapsulates his view of himself and his life with cerebral palsy. David continues to believe that God is sovereign in His decisions about our lives. God has designed every baby "fearfully and wonderfully" before the foundation of the world, and He doesn't define *normal* the way we do.

> *People come up to me and say, "Brother Dave, don't you want to be normal?"*
>
> *I look at them and say, "What's normal? You think you're normal? You have a long way to go! Some of you are not going to make it!"*
>
> *I don't want to be normal; I want to be just like God made me. I don't know about you, but my God doesn't make junk. . . . I thank God for giving me the privilege of being born with cerebral palsy so that God's glory can be shown in my life.*

Not long after their marriage the Rings themselves were confronted with the issue of "normal" or "perfect" babies. Even before their wedding, Karen and David had been warned by friends and family that they shouldn't get their hopes up about having children. If they decided to be parents, who knew what kind of tragedy might occur? The risks of heartbreak seemed too great.

During David's youth, a doctor had advised him that he probably could not father children, although no tests or scientific evidence were given to support that unhappy diagnosis. Furthermore, if his wife did conceive, some people expressed the fear that they would inherit David's handicap. Of course, medically speaking, that was impossible. Cerebral palsy is the result of damage at birth or just before. David's condition was due to oxygen deprivation, not heredity. Yet the warnings were voiced again and again.

Casting caution to the wind, Karen and David continued to dream about a family. Karen had been surrounded by babies and toddlers as a teenager; both she and her mother made extra money caring for other people's children. David was well aware of his fiancée's love for children; in fact, his heart was touched when he saw how lovingly she responded to them. Even before their marriage, David and Karen chose names for their first child: Joshua, if he were a boy and April, if she were a girl.

Just as David had been discouraged about marriage, family members also had reminded him that he would surely disappoint a wife as far as childbearing was concerned. Again, their intention was to protect him from disappointment, but he turned a deaf ear. The warnings may have troubled him, but they didn't stop him from believing that "all things are possible with God." Besides, the new Mr. and Mrs. Ring had already decided to wait a little while before starting a family. There was plenty of time to pray for a miracle.

Five weeks after the wedding, Karen was at a revival with David. "I remember getting sick driving to lunch and wondering what was wrong," she said. A week later, after Karen had visited the family doctor, David got a phone call.

"I was in Memphis, Tennessee, doing a revival. Karen called me at my motel. 'Hi, Daddy,' was all she had to say. I didn't even know she had gone to the doctor. I still cannot explain in words what happened. It was as if one more time God said, 'I'm in control. I'm the one calling the shots.'"

David and Karen fell in love all over again. The pregnancy was breathing more life into their already vital relationship. In their eyes, the pregnancy was another confirmation of God's favor upon their marriage. Truly He had blessed them beyond all they could ask or think.

Of course, as they always do, friends began to make comments and ask questions.

"What do you want? A boy or girl? I bet you don't care what it is as long as it's healthy!"

"What does the doctor think?"

"Is there any danger of something not being right?"

"What causes C.P. anyway?"

David Ring was born into a family that had been plagued with tragedy and handicaps. He had long ago settled with himself the false assumption that only "healthy" people were lovable, acceptable, or welcome. He listened to the words of well-meaning individuals. But his answer to questions about the first child was always the same: "We'll be happy with whatever baby the Lord gives us."

David was in Oklahoma to lead a revival when he received the phone call Sunday at 8:00 A.M. "I thought it was a wake-up call. It was Karen. Her water [bag] had broken—she was in labor. I called the preacher and told him I couldn't make it. I didn't even begin the revival.

"I flew back home to St. Charles and got there at about 12:30 in the afternoon. Karen had been in the hospital, but they had sent her home. By mid-afternoon Karen was in so much pain with her contractions that I insisted on taking her back to the hospital. We got there around 3:00 P.M.; our little baby girl came at 2:58 the next morning.

"April Jane was born June 21, 1982. June 21 is the longest day of the year—and that was especially true for Karen in 1982."

People who came to the hospital were amazed. Friends of the Rings said, time and again, "I don't know what it is—there's something special about April."

David smiles, still shaking his head in wonder. "She was a gift from God. That's all I can say. I really bonded with April. I was so excited that she was my own flesh."

God had indeed given the Rings the desire of their hearts. That's not to say that every precaution wasn't taken to insure April's health. Karen ate carefully. She exercised regularly. But, as she explains, April's well-being was really God's decision all along. In retrospect, Karen observes:

"We knew that God had already formed April Jane, and she was fearfully and wonderfully made by His hand. We were only the means He chose to send her through. She was beautiful, by no stretch of the imagination, and the epitome of all a mom and dad could want. Beautiful dark hair. Big brown eyes. She was soon to become her Daddy's pride and joy."

David's shaky hands made him afraid to hold his first baby. Instead of taking the chance of picking her up and either crushing or dropping her, he sat in a blue bedroom chair with a pillow on his lap, where he lovingly cradled her. As he watched her perfect form and movements, he could hardly believe his eyes.

April Jane Ring was dedicated to the One who made her perfect, healthy, and "normal" at the same church where her parents met and were married—First Baptist Church, St. Charles, Missouri. Karen, David, and April Jane stood as a family in front of a joyful, weeping congregation as their pastor, Jay Piper, prayed God's blessing upon the first Ring infant.

Ashley Dawn, the Ring's second child, was born February 26, 1985. As was the case with all four children, David was holding a revival when he got the call that Karen had gone into labor. This time he was in Avon Park, Florida. The phone rang at 11:00 on a Monday night, and he couldn't find a flight home until 6:00 the following morning.

"I'll never make it home on time," he grumbled to himself, frantic to be at Karen's side. His flight landed at 10:30 the next morning; Ashley was born at 2:14 that afternoon.

Again, the child was beautiful in face and form. The Rings rejoiced once more at the goodness of God. They had not prayed for perfection; they had only asked God to give them the baby of His choosing.

Before their third child was born, the Rings moved to Orlando. It happened this way: During the Pastors' Conference in Atlanta, Jim Henry, pastor of the First Baptist Church of Orlando, introduced himself to David. "Next time you're in town," he said, "please come speak at our church." David spoke the following year, and he and Jim became fast friends. Jim soon began his attempts to convince David to move to Florida and become the staff evangelist at First Baptist Church. Eventually, in 1987, the Rings relocated.

Each Ring baby interrupted a revival, but according to David's calculations Nathan cost more in airline tickets than in hospital charges.

By the time baby number three was about to come into the world, April was in kindergarten, and the family had been enjoying a school festival. Karen was uncomfortably pregnant but chose to walk around with David and the girls all Saturday afternoon. She was more than ready to have the pregnancy finished—maybe walking would speed things up. David was to fly to Dallas that night to start a revival in Longview, Texas, the next morning. As she told him good-bye at the gate, Karen said, "Don't be alarmed, but I'm having contractions."

"Do you want me to stay?"

"No, it's probably false labor. Go ahead."

David flew to Dallas. When he called home upon arrival at Dallas-Ft. Worth airport, Karen said, "Sorry, but it's the real thing."

David got back on the same plane, buckled himself into the same seat, and smiled at the same flight attendant. He got to Orlando at 11:00 the same night and found Karen at home. Her contractions had stopped. The baby wasn't coming after all.

Karen was devastated. David comforted her as well as he could, and spent Saturday night at home. Sunday afternoon he flew back to Dallas and drove directly to the big tent that marked the location of the Longview crusade. He preached Sunday and Monday nights. On Tuesday morning at 6:30 the phone rang. It was Karen. "I'm in labor," she announced meekly.

David was back in Orlando before noon. Nathan was born that afternoon—May 10, 1988. Once the baby had safely entered the world, David flew back to Longview and finished the crusade the next day.

Their fourth child was the closest call of all. David nearly missed Amy Joy's birth on March 22, 1990. He received the phone call just as he was about to preach in South Carolina. *Karen has long labors,* he told himself, and he decided to go ahead with the sermon. Afterward, he caught the first available flight home, which was the last flight of the day. When he arrived in Atlanta to change planes, he called the Orlando hospital.

"You're not going to make it," he was told. His heart sank. *I shouldn't have tried to preach,* he chastised himself.

His plane landed in Orlando at 1:05 A.M. He rushed into the hospital at 1:30. Amy was born at 1:36. Even the doctor was stunned when David burst into the delivery room in the nick of time.

David laughs about the commuter deliveries. He believes that God has used his preaching to bring the miracle of his children's births to the awareness of thousands of people. "Keep in mind that I'm with churches every time a baby comes. Those churches witness the miracle. They experience the miracle. Every baby is testimony to them of the power of God."

Although being an evangelist is his calling and his passion, David Ring is first and foremost a family man. Perhaps it is because of the wonder he still feels at the sight of his children—children that weren't supposed to be possible and certainly weren't expected to be quite so beautiful. Maybe, too, his dedication to being a good daddy is due to his affection for his own father, reflecting the respect for Oscar Ring he still holds in his heart.

David lost his father when he was just a young boy, but when David became a preacher, people who remembered Oscar's old-time religion style of evangelism were stunned. His son David, who hadn't seen his dad since his eleventh year, was displaying the same mannerisms, the same gestures, the same intense way of presenting the gospel message.

David is immensely loyal to his father's memory. He fondly remembers sitting in the front row of a little country church, transfixed by Oscar's sermons. He recalls the man, dressed in bib overalls, with one arm missing, beckoning his listeners to give their hearts to Jesus, to receive salvation from the fire and brimstone of hell. Being both a preacher and a good father is part of David Ring's heritage, and Oscar's faithfulness is never far from his heart as he travels the United States, preaching the same gospel Daddy preached so many years ago.

When April was nearly a year old, in April 1983, David was called to hold a revival in a small Georgia town called Fitzgerald. It was a sleepy place, and although everyone was looking forward to hearing David Ring speak, no one anticipated anything out of the ordinary. Yet God had something in store for His son David—something that would keep him looking heavenward for the rest of his life.

"The preacher and I entered through a side door, and we came up on the platform and took our seats on a bench," David begins. "The music evangelist got up at 11:00 A.M. sharp and started singing, and we began the revival. When he started singing and when people started singing with him, I began crying. The song ended, and I was bawling like a baby."

David is not sure why he started to cry. It is not his nature. "My wife can tell you, I don't cry," David continues. "I wish I did. It's not easy for me to cry. But that morning I cried more than I had in a long time. I looked at the preacher, and he was crying, too. He poked me and said, 'Hang on, something's about to happen. I don't know what, but hang on.'

"I said, 'I'm hangin', man.'

"It was my turn, and I got up to speak and told my life story. I said, 'I don't know why I'm crying, but I thank God that I am, because tears are the language only God understands.'

"Everybody else was crying by then, too. I gave my life story the best I knew how, and I sang the song 'Victory in Jesus,' like I always do. When I finished singing, it all came together.

"A man in the back of the auditorium stood up. He only had one arm. He didn't say anything out loud, but my heart heard him: 'Son, I'm proud of you. I'm proud to be your daddy.'

"I couldn't take my eyes off the man, and when he'd finished saying that he turned away and went out the double doors. When he got through those doors he turned around. I heard him in my heart again, saying, 'Son, see you later. It won't be long. Gotta go now.' He turned and went out.

"I didn't see that man again that week, but I know who it was. He was my daddy. My daddy came to hear me preach in 1983. Maybe you're saying, 'What do you mean, it's your daddy? You had a vision.'

"It wasn't a vision. All week long, people were asking each other, 'Did you see the man? Did you see him? Does anybody know where that man lives? That man had one arm. That man had a glow on his face. Does anybody know who that man was?'"

Was it his father? No one in the little town of Fitzgerald could identify the one-armed man. David, though, knew his dad had visited him once more, perhaps to give his blessing on the ministry.

"I didn't say anything until Wednesday night," David continues. "That night I said that my daddy had come to church Sunday morning. The church came unglued. God saved eighty-seven people in four days."

Sometimes, when David preaches about heaven, he tells another story, a story of a nearly fatal day in May 1986. He tells it to emphasize how close we are to heaven at every moment.

Karen and he had been working outside, tending the garden that surrounded their backyard swimming pool. Karen went to the market and left April playing in the pool under David's supervision. April was wearing an inflatable winged horse, which kept her afloat. Impulsively, she took it off, running around the pool without it.

"Put it back on, April," David warned her.

He watched her obediently tugging at it, not realizing that she had not managed to get it back on completely. Absorbed in his work, he turned around moments later to see his firstborn child lying on her back, in the deep end of the pool, and floating a foot underwater. Her eyes were open. She appeared to be dead.

His heart nearly exploding with fear, David jumped into the pool with his clothes on. He grabbed her and shook her. "April, April! Talk to Daddy!"

He tugged, pulled, and lifted his three-year-old out of the pool. "April, April! Talk to daddy. Talk to daddy!" But April did not respond to David's words. She wasn't moving. She wasn't breathing.

No one on earth understood better than David the danger of oxygen deprivation to a small child. He shook April, called to her, pleaded with her to hear him. A next-door neighbor who was working outside heard David's frenzied appeals. He jumped over the fence. Scooping April up from David's arms, he abruptly turned her upside down and patted her firmly on the back.

With a choking sound, April started crying. She looked at David and said, "Oh, Daddy! Hold me."

David called the hospital. "Bring her in immediately," he was firmly instructed. "She may still have water in her lungs. There's still a possibility of brain damage."

As April lay on the emergency room examination table, the doctors asked various questions, most of which she did not answer. "What is your name?" "How old are you?" The little girl simply stared at them in shock.

David and Karen were terrified. April had always been such a bright little girl. Her vocabulary was that of an adult and had been so since her second birthday. Traveling had further broadened her world, and those who met her were always amazed at her maturity and ability to communicate. The thought of damage to her brain was almost too much to bear.

It seemed as if an eternity had come and gone before April finally spoke. By then she was lying in her hospital bed. All at once she sat up and said, "Daddy, I'm hungry. Will you get me a McDonald's Happy Meal?" She had come out of shock and was now a normal little girl, remembering McDonald's and getting hungry.

David was off in a flash, ready to purchase a million Happy Meals, so grateful was his heart.

April's relieved parents stayed at the hospital with her all night. David was so shaken that he couldn't bear to leave her side. The next morning the doctor sent the family home. As they gathered their things, he said to David, "You are a very lucky man."

David, his face still drawn with stress, answered, "There's no such word in my vocabulary. I'm blessed by God."

The doctor nodded and added, "Ten more seconds and your little girl would have been dead."

Ten seconds. Today, when he tells the story to congregations all over America, David counts the seconds out. "Ten, nine, eight, seven, six, five, four, three, two, one. Where will you be?" he asks. "Heaven? Or hell?"

The hospital team gave April a clean bill of health, and David left that same day for a revival. He was unprepared for the agony he felt as he boarded the plane. He felt as if he were being separated from his child for the rest of his life. That weekend he could not look at anyone without crying. The revival was going well, but the memory of his daughter's brush with heaven haunted him.

Heaven. His own daddy was there, and he knew it well. His momma was there, too, and he looked forward to a joyful reunion with her one day. But April Jane Ring? She was David's miracle child—his firstborn, his proof of God's power, his evidence of God's miraculous love. He wasn't ready to tell her good-bye or to watch her struggle with the damage she might have suffered from oxygen loss. David was devastated by the near-tragedy. But in the midst of it, he was once again faced with a sovereign Lord, who gives and takes, who is the master of life and death who, in His justice, always remembers mercy.

While David marvels at their near perfection, his children are almost totally unaware of his handicaps. When April was five years old, she sat watching her father hard at work at the kitchen table. She stared a long time, noticing that his hands shook as he wrote and remarked, "Mom, Dad doesn't write very good. It's really messy."

Just as Karen prepared to answer with a careful explanation about David's cerebral palsy, April continued, "That's OK, Dad. All boys write that way."

Nathan probably best summed up the children's view of their father during one father-son outing to McDonald's. David pulled the family car into a handicapped parking place and took the Florida handicapped driver tag out of the glove box to place it in view.

"Dad, why are you parking in the handicapped space?" Nathan shook his head in dismay. "You aren't handicapped. You shouldn't be parking here."

Nevertheless, there is never a day that David Ring isn't aware of his dependence upon God's grace. He sees it when he looks into the eyes of his wife and children. He remembers it when he recalls the love of his faithful mother, and the friendly wave of the one-armed visitor in the Georgia revival. He is reminded of it as he reads the letters that come to him from parents—parents of children who battled, as he has always battled, with cerebral palsy. His struggle is his own; theirs is a war against their children's pain. Who can say which is more difficult?

Dear Evangelist Ring,

I thought I'd write to you to say I watched and listened to your video tape. My name is Charlene and I have a sixteen year old son who has cerebral palsy. He doesn't talk. Doctors say he cannot hear. Over the years they told me he would not live to be five or twenty five. I believe in the Lord Jesus. I was baptized when I was twelve.

I believe my son Tommy does hear and will talk someday. I was inspired so much by your tape. I'm going to let my son Tommy watch your tape. I believe he will watch and listen to you. I hope for my son to meet you sometime. The doctors had also said he would not walk but he did in April 1986.

I praise God and am thankful everyday for Tommy. He has inspired so many lives. I have not given up hope and I won't. I am sending you a picture of him. So pray for Tommy and my family.

May God bless you and your family.

One family realized that they had been limiting God in their prayers for their son who had C.P. They prayed for both of their children every day, but until they heard David, they prayed for each one differently. They asked God to use their bright five-year-old daughter in a mighty way; yet for their son they asked only that God would make life easier for him and that people would accept him. They knew his limited potential. At least they thought they did.

We assumed that God could use Kimberly, a healthy, whole being, for His glory, but could not use Jacob with all of his limitations.

Then we met David Ring.

I saw God mightily using you—a man who struggled in many of the same areas as Jacob. I saw God using those limitations in ways that were limitless. I was convicted that my faithless prayers for Jacob all along were setting limits on God's ability.

Now our prayers for our two children are identical: "God take their lives with all their potential, whether it seems great or small to us, and use them to glorify you and Your Kingdom."

God may not choose to use Jacob in the same way that He is using you, but I now know that there are no limitations on a life that is yielded to and used by God.

Another woman had two children. Her two-year-old was active and outgoing, and her older child, Ashley, was shy and gentle—and had cerebral palsy. Ashley learned to walk with crutches and loved to sing. The Lord blessed her with a beautiful voice. She wrote David:

There are times when I look at Ashley and see the struggles and disappointments that she faces and the ones that lie ahead for her. It becomes overwhelming for me. I have been struggling lately more so than ever before. I am trying to concentrate on the Lord and grow closer to Him. He has brought us through so very much. My husband and I have mentioned to others how we praise God for Ashley Dawn and the cerebral palsy and how the Lord is using her to touch so many lives. He has used her tremendously ever since he wonderfully and fearfully made her four years and nine months ago. Unless one is saved they do not understand what my husband and I mean by this.

Thank you David Ring for the very special blessing that the Lord has made you in our lives. You and your wonderful family are in our prayers.

Karen has her own thoughts about parenthood and family life. She reflects upon David as a husband and father:

"All of us have many roles we play in life. So does David Ring. Some, mostly those of the world who do not know Christ, see David as a crippled man, one with a most visible handicap. But to those who have heard him speak, he is a powerful preacher of the gospel.

"To me, he is much more than that. He is my dearest friend, my closest companion, the one I have chosen to invest myself in, and with whom I share my life on earth.

"David has seen me at my best and at my worst. He has loved me just the same. His tender touch and soft words have encouraged me when I thought my world was caving in. Yet I have experienced his strong voice of authority in times when we were facing great decisions.

"David is God's choice man for me.

"To the children, he is their friend—one who will listen to them. Whether he is at home or on the road, he always makes himself available to them. Some days they have nothing to say, but they know he's there. He is always ready to help with homework, to swim in the pool, or to watch a good movie.

"Sometimes I think David is the biggest kid of all. However, despite his playfulness, he somehow manages to hold that firm, strong hand of authority in the household. He has strong convictions on discipline and respect for authority, yet he manages to find a good balance between love and discipline.

"Above anything else, beyond anything David says or does with the children, they know one thing: they know that they are loved unconditionally by their dad. And that's what really counts."

10

HIDDEN HANDICAPS

David Ring likes to compare the struggles of life to the game of baseball. Maybe it's because baseball is his favorite sport; maybe its because everyone has struggles in life, just as they do playing sports. During one sermon, David explained the similarities this way:

My favorite sport is baseball. When I was eight or nine years old, I played Little League baseball. I was so thrilled to be able to participate. I had my little uniform and wore it proudly. Every accomplishment I made in my life was a big deal.

I recall one particular game. After an inning, I was taking my position in left field. As I was walking between shortstop and left field, I tripped and fell. Everyone emptied the stands to see if I was all right. My momma was the first one there as usual. She ran out to pick me up and see if I was OK. Looking back, I'm amazed at how many people protected me all the time.

I wasn't hurt, but it sure scared a lot of folks.

At a baseball park, we hear those resounding words "S-t-r-i-k-e one, s-t-r-i-k-e two, s-t-r-i-k-e three! You're out!"

Those are depressing words to a player. They are the words of defeat. That was exactly the way it was in my own life.

I had three strikes against me.

Strike one, I was born with cerebral palsy.

Strike two, I lost my daddy.

Strike three, I lost my momma.

I was "out" in every sense of the word. I was heading for the dugout with my head tucked down. The game was over as far as I was concerned.

Then, all of a sudden, my life was touched by God, the greatest Coach in all the world. His touch put me back in the game of life.

I had been a nobody, rejected by everyone, and I had no purpose. He took my lonely, crippled life, just as He took the little boy's lunch in John chapter six. It wasn't much, but it was all the little boy had.

That is all Jesus requires of us. If we give Him all we are, He will take us as we are. It may not be much, but He will take us anyway.

I gave Him a hopeless and lonely life, but He took it. After He took it, He blessed it beyond measure, just as He did with the five loaves and two fish. He blesses everything He takes.

After I gave my life to Him, He turned it around. He changed everything. He gave me a precious family and a wonderful ministry. His isn't just a one-time blessing; it is daily. And He does the same thing for others. He watches over all His children all the time.

David is constantly aware of God's continuous blessing. Yet for a man or woman with David's particular difficulties, daily living can be a wearisome business. Without the help of the "greatest Coach in all the world," David's lot in life would be all but impossible to bear.

Every step David takes, every word he speaks, and every bite he eats requires more than double a normal person's concentration and effort. Uncooperative muscles have to be constantly at the command of his mind. He must fight to perform, and that fight is never won without physical pain and exhaustion.

In addition, the kinds of things that go wrong in the lives of ordinary people go wrong for David Ring too. He has to cope with commonplace troubles, just like everyone else. Take, for example, the night in 1982 when he and Jim McNiel visited a convenience store in Louisville, Kentucky.

They had been holding a revival, and they had stopped by the store to pick up some sodas on their way back to the hotel. A video game caught their attention, and they popped a couple of quarters into the machine to try their luck. Just as the game lit up, two masked gunmen rushed into the store.

One of them pointed a gun at David's head and shouted, "Throw me your wallet."

In the stress of the moment, David completely lost his sense of hearing. "Throw me your wallet!" The man ordered a second time. David finally understood and threw his wallet across the room.

Jim was praying, "God, help him throw it straight!" He was terrified that, with his shaky hands, David might hurl the wallet halfway across the room, enraging the assailants.

Fortunately, it went directly to the robber. Unfortunately, it contained a substantial amount of money, a large loss to David's family.

Three days later, back at home, David was taking care of some routine responsibilities with Karen. All at once, he started weeping—an unusual occurrence for him, except in the wake of a major upheaval.

"What's wrong?" Karen asked, shocked at his sudden emotional reaction. They quickly realized that he was still suffering the trauma of the robbery. It stayed with him for months.

In 1988, another frightening incident occurred. It could have happened to anyone, but in the face of his other difficulties, it was especially shattering to David.

During summer storms, Florida roads are infamous for what locals call "Florida black ice," which is a dangerous layer of slippery oil, brought to the surface by heavy rain.

One August afternoon, David and his family were about one hundred miles outside Orlando when he lost control of the car. It spun around, rolled over three times, and finally landed on its top. The roof on the driver's side was completely smashed. The car was a total loss.

The family was deeply shaken, but, miraculously, no one was hurt. In fact, four hours after the accident, David was preaching. Even though the brush with death had nothing to do with David's cerebral palsy, it was another time when the usual stresses and strains of life almost brought him to the breaking point. Yet he realizes that God uses brokenness to bless His children, as he pointed out during one sermon:

> *After Jesus blesses something, He breaks it. It is a humbling thing to be blessed by God. It brings brokenness every time. A person can't be blessed by God without being broken by Him. God loves a broken and contrite heart.*
>
> *As God's children, we are in a breaking process daily. We have things in our lives that God uses to break us. Sometimes they are obvious, and sometimes they are hidden handicaps. We cover them up by acting as though everything is all right. I may be all right on the outside, but it is another story on the inside.*

Sometimes we look at brokenness negatively. The enemy wants us to view it that way. The devil means it for evil, but God means it for good.

Why do bad things happen to God's people? So that God's glory can be seen in that situation. God uses things in our lives to conform us to the image of His Son.

If God hadn't taken my momma away, I would still be in Arkansas pulling on her apron strings. Now I am in Orlando, Florida, pulling on God's grace. My dependence went from my momma to God. God's grace is surely sufficient. We throw away broken things, but God doesn't. He uses broken things. When He breaks us, He can use us.

David Ring talks about two kinds of brokenness. One is physical or emotional brokenness that renders an individual "useless" in the eyes of the world. As David frequently points out, God is able to turn that kind of circumstance around for His glory and our good.

Spiritual brokenness, on the other hand, is a place every Christian must reach in order to realize his or her need for God. That brokenness makes us both dependent on and useful to Him.

David is well aware of the various aspects of his own brokenness, and he has become comfortable with them. In fact, the ability to laugh at himself is probably the most indisputable proof of his changed inner life. There was a time when embarrassing experiences propelled him into the depths of despair. Today he knows that "God is not finished with me yet," and that makes all the difference in his responses.

All my life I've been made fun of because of cerebral palsy. It used to bother me. It doesn't bother me anymore because God is not finished with me yet. They still make fun of me. You wouldn't believe what I go through in life. I went to Atlanta one time. I got off the plane, and a guy came up to me and poked me on the shoulder. "Excuse me, have you had a little too much to drink?"

I said, "No! I'm a Baptist preacher."

"Sure you are, man," the guy said. It took me ten minutes to convince him I wasn't drunk.

Another time I was in Detroit, on my way to Alabama to do a revival. I gave the lady at the gate my ticket. All I said was "Good morning, how are you?" She gave me my boarding pass. But before she gave it to me she wrote on it, "Mentally retarded."

And I took it. I thought, Well, that's cool. When I woke up this morning, two hours ago, I looked in the mirror, and I didn't look retarded. But maybe in two hours' time, mental retardation set in. So I thought, Well, I'm going to go along for the ride.

They told me to sit down, so I sat down.

They ushered me on board before anybody else. I like that.

They sat me down on the plane and fastened my seat belt for me. So far so good.

Finally everybody got on board, and we took off.

Then they came to me again and asked me something. Have you ever noticed how somebody talks to a mental retarded guy? They get right up in your face. And they talk loudly.

She said, "Do you want a Coke!"

I said, "Huh?"

"Do you want a Coke!"

"Huh?"

Finally she brought me a Coke.

When we landed they came to me and said, "Keep your seat until everybody gets off." Everybody got off, and they came and got me.

When we got to the terminal, there stood a man with a wheelchair—for me. I thought, That's cool. Since I got up I became retarded. Number two, I can't use my hands.

Number three, I'm deaf. Now I'm lame. Keep on going, I'll be dead.

They told me to sit down; I sat down. And away we went. When we finally got to the gate I jumped up, took my bag and walked off. I took about four steps, turned around, and looked at the man that pushed me, whose mouth was wide open. I said, "By the way, I'm not retarded."

You say, "David, doesn't that bother you?"

No. Because God is not finished with me yet.

The fact that all Christians are in the process of being transformed is central to David's preaching. He realizes that no matter how healthy we may look on the outside, none of us is really "normal." We all have hidden handicaps. We are all crippled in some areas and blind, deaf, or mute in others.

Eating is one of the most difficult activities in David's life. His fine motor skills constantly challenge him. It is hard to balance food on a shaky fork. It is difficult to get all the food or drink into his mouth without spilling. Early in his ministry, David learned the hard way that it is almost impossible not to break a fine bone china cup and saucer, proudly brought out by a well-meaning hostess—especially when she is nervously scrutinizing every clattering, shaky move.

Before his life was touched by God, David would not eat in the presence of anyone except family. Today, as with every other area of his existence, he has learned to live within the limitations of his disability.

The only time anyone will be truly healthy is in heaven, at the climax of God's transformation process, when we leave this flawed, earthly life and enter the next realm of eternity. Perhaps that is why belief in heaven is so dear to David's heart. Heaven represents healing, wholeness, and freedom from continuous struggle.

I don't know what it's like to have a normal body. I'm glad I don't know what it's like to have a normal body be-

cause one day I'm going to have a perfect body. Not only will I walk like Him, not only will I talk like Him, but I'm going to eat like Him.

"What do you mean, 'eat like Him'?"

What's wrong when I eat? When I eat, I shake. When I preach, I don't shake too much. But when you eat with me, watch out for flying food. I have to sneak up on my glass of water to get a drink.

But don't feel sorry for me. Don't say, "Poor David, he can't eat well." I get the job done.

One day, thank God, one day I'm going to walk up to a banquet table without shaking. And I'm going to be able to sit there, and I'm going to be able to eat just like the King of kings and Lord of lords.

God never ceases to remind David Ring, and those close to him, that His strength is made perfect in weakness. Although victory in Jesus is always the outcome, the struggle is continuous. In that battle, David is profoundly aware that the weaknesses that cause him such difficulty are the tools God uses to bring others to Himself.

Because his mind is bright and his intuition quick, David is easily frustrated by his inability to communicate his deepest thoughts and to speak eloquently. He is quick to note, with a sheepish grin, that "the foolish things of the world confound the wise." It is abundantly clear that his speech impediment has caused more people to come to Christ than any other aspect of his presentation of the gospel. And, strange as it may seem, he has concluded that the television remote control is a vital key to his particular success as well.

"People sit at home, or in motels or hotels, flipping through the channels. When they hear my voice, they wonder who it is and why he's talking that way. They stop and listen. God uses my words and the way I talk to touch their hearts.

"I remember when my family and I were on vacation in the Washington, D.C., area. We were leaving Arlington

Cemetery, and I stopped to ask a guard directions to our motel.

"He didn't answer for a few seconds. I assumed he didn't hear or couldn't understand me. So I repeated myself.

"The man started crying. I thought, *What in the world did I say?*

"Finally he said, 'I can't believe my eyes. I saw you on TV two months ago, and God changed my life. I ordered your video and sent it to my mother. She got saved because of your video.'

"I've heard the same story repeated in airports, restaurants, and on the streets."

God, of course, knows all about TV remote controls, and He has always had plans to get David Ring coast-to-coast television exposure. As a result of this TV exposure, invitations have come from churches, schools, and business institutions. As is often the case, God's plans involved some unexpected preparations. In fact, He did something particularly significant in David Ring's ministry in 1988, which set the stage for what would later become a national ministry. David cites it as a classic example of walking by faith. "I was really taking a faith step when I called Danny de Armas."

For nearly seven years David had longed for someone who could relieve him of the administrative aspects of his ministry. He began to pray, earnestly and continuously, about that need. "All I wanted to do was preach, be with my family, and study. I needed someone who was gifted in areas where I wasn't."

In the early part of the year, David held a revival in New Port Richey, Florida, where a young man named Danny de Armas was an associate pastor. The church assigned Danny the responsibility of caring for David throughout the week.

David recalls, "I told my wife on the phone that Danny was the sharpest twenty-five-year-old man I'd ever met."

On Wednesday night, the two men talked about their lives. Danny asked David, "What do you want to do? Where will your ministry go?"

David explained that he was frustrated with the way churches publicized his revivals. "I have a big crowd on Sunday, but on Monday night the bottom falls out. I really need somebody who can promote a revival. Somebody who will make sure I have a good crowd the whole week."

The two men enjoyed each other's fellowship during that particular crusade. When David returned home, he didn't mention the possibility of Danny's involvement to Karen, although the thought had crossed his mind more than once. But by that summer, David knew in his heart what he had to do. He stepped out in faith and called Danny.

David uses the story as an example of his faith walk:

"We walk by faith and not by sight. If you get a direct command from the Lord, He'll make the way for everybody. Danny is like Aaron to me, when he held Moses' arms up. Danny has the spiritual gift of helps. He dots every *i* and crosses every *t*. And we've never once had to worry about our financial commitment to him. Once we stepped out in faith, the money has always been there."

It is evident that Danny's involvement with David was indeed part of the Father's plan. Soon after he teamed up with David, another bend in the road brought David into the national eye. He needed all the administrative help he could get.

In late 1988, a member of Jerry Falwell's staff heard David's testimony and invited him to Lynchburg, Virginia, to preach.

"I'd love to come," David responded enthusiastically. He suddenly recalled an impression he had had years before. In 1971, just after God had called him to preach, he had seen Jerry Falwell on television. *I want to be with that man someday*, he thought suddenly.

On a Sunday night in January 1989, David Ring preached at Thomas Road Baptist Church. Although David didn't know that Jerry Falwell would be there, he was present—and he was deeply moved. He invited David to stay and speak at the college chapel at Liberty University the following Monday morning. He said to his scheduling team, "Whatever you do, book David to come back on a Sunday morning."

David spoke on Jerry Falwell's national television broadcast in September 1989. Fortunately, Danny de Armas was already in place to handle the avalanche of opportunities that came as a result. As it was, the two of them could not answer all the phone calls. Following his first appearance on coast-to-coast television, David Ring received thirty-eight speaking invitations in five days.

One of several powerful messages David Ring has since preached in the Lynchburg pulpit offers his perspective on hidden handicaps and illustrates why he is able to reach people in a unique and dramatic way. It's more than a sermon— it's an object lesson. He appears at the podium well dressed and begins a rather startling process of removing items of clothing. By the time he's finished, the message is clear: "Quit worrying about what people think about you on the outside. Just worry about what God thinks about you on the inside."

> *Let me give you an illustration: How many of you think I look good? Is my suit OK? Do I look good? Do you like my tie? I love my tie. I picked it out. I look OK, don't I?*
>
> *Well, let me tell you, if you think I look OK, you've been taken to the cleaners.*
>
> *You say, "David, you look fine."*
>
> *But you only see what's on the outside. I know what's on the inside. For example, what if I take off my shoes?*

David removes his shoes, and he's wearing two unmatched, holey socks. His toes are sticking out of them. "Can you believe I came to church like this?" he asks. "What if I keep going?"

He takes off his jacket, and his shirt sleeves are cut off raggedly. "Now what do I look like?"

When he takes off his vest, the true state of his tie is revealed. It is only long enough to look presentable when the rest of his suit is in place. He has chopped off the bottom unevenly.

By the time David has finished disrobing, he is standing in rags and tatters behind the pulpit. "Don't we come to church like this?" he continues. "Don't we come to church and put on our Sunday go-to-meeting clothes and say, 'I'm OK. I'm OK. I'm OK'? But God is saying, 'No! I see you for what you really are!'"

No cover-up can disguise David's affliction. His weaknesses are too obvious to hide. His problems are public domain, evident for all the world to see. Yet his ministry is not limited to those who are similarly disabled. He also speaks to the private battles, the secret frailties, and the hidden handicaps of every man and woman.

David Ring knows that only heaven—certainly not earth—will be populated with perfect, strong, normal people. Until then, he assures all who will listen that God's strength is more than sufficient to see us through, no matter how helpless we are.

As David reflects upon his ministry, he says, " My idea of a revival is more than seeing souls saved from hell. Salvation isn't just a rescue from eternal damnation. It's also an ongoing work, which allows God to save us from defeat in our daily lives. Salvation means being more than conquerors in Him, both in this life and in the life to come.

"Ephesians 4:12 calls us all to build up the body of Christ. My philosophy is that when the family of God is built up and encouraged, they are going to do the work of evangelism. Everyone is called to be an evangelist, and we have to build up each other."

David's challenge to men and women, boys and girls has changed hearts all over America. People instinctively understand that he knows that life can be difficult. They recognize that he is not judgmental. They respond to his appeal for inner truth and outward commitment by walking forward in churches, bowing their heads in prayer in homes and hotel rooms, and accepting the truth of the gospel from the lips of someone who has been there.

The results pour into Orlando, expressed in letters of gratitude, hope, and longing. They are addressed to the one person who was able to break through the authors' self-pity. He accomplishes that with his simple command to stop asking why and to start asking what. "What can I do to glorify God with my problems?"

Dear Reverend David Ring,

Tuesday I felt down. I was having seizures—8 in one day. I called the preacher and said, "pray for me." I told him my life is ruined. I have always had cerebral palsy. He came down and he brought a videotape of one of your sermons with Jerry Falwell. My heart was so heavy. I watched the tape. God called you to preach. I told the preacher I wanted to be baptized. I accepted Christ that night when I saw your tape. That Sunday I joined the church, on the 27 of March. When I walked up the aisle, everybody cried.

One thirty-four-year-old man with cerebral palsy wrote about his experience. He heard David on the New Inspirational Network and knew that he would understand.

People always made fun of me, and still do. Only if they understood my condition! Even though I have got cerebral palsy and have seizures every now and then, I am able to buy my share of the groceries, buy my clothes, help pay on the utilities and the phone bill.

> I still talk slow. I cannot run, hop or even skip. Neither can I drive. I am still praying that will change. I just thank God for blessing me. Also, in a way healing me. I could have ended up being worse. I love you David. I will be praying for you. Please also pray for me daily.

One woman contacted David after suffering the deaths of her husband and father within four months.

> Brother Ring,
> Thank you so very much for the letter I just received this morning. Sweet words of comfort do help so much, so very uplifting. I could never have made it through these hard times . . . if hadn't been for the prayers of God's saints bearing my burdens up to God. And oh, what a joy it was to get your video. It is truly marvelous. God did not make a mistake when He made you just as you are. In fact He made a great man.

One man in Christian work was wrestling with his own internal struggles. He seldom stayed home during the day or watched TV, but one day he happened to catch one of David's broadcasts.

> At first I wanted to turn it off, but something said I should listen. . . . I have been afraid to give [my struggles] to God and have depended upon my strengths. When

I heard your message and saw your life, God was speaking to me. It confirmed that God can love me no matter what. And that he wants to use my wounds to show His glory. After hearing you I sat in my room and asked God to take my wounds and use me to bring Him glory. David, I want to be like you.

Thank you for being an example of a person who believes and depends on God. To God be the Glory, great things He has done. Thanks for your testimony that says that even if others don't believe in us, God never gives up on us!

The letters come from young and old, educated and uneducated. Whether listening to the evangelist on a televison broadcast, a videotape, or an audio recording, viewers and listeners find David's story inspiring and often decide to pray for his ministry. Sometimes the letters are warm, personal, and even humorous.

Dear Mr. David Ring,

I really like your movie and your tapes. Also, Victory in Jesus is one of my favorit songs, too! I injoy listing to your tapes very much. I also like watching your movie. I love your messages you tell. They are relly strong and incurging. How is your family? Well I must go now. God bless you and keep you safe.

The packed church is silent but for the sound of muffled sobs and the quiet rustling of tissues as tearful eyes are wiped. As David Ring brings his sermon to a close, not a person is present who hasn't been moved—deeply moved—by his words.

Not one person in the sanctuary arrived without a handicap. Whether that handicap is physical, mental, or spiritual, David Ring has asked every person listening to him to overcome, not to succumb. Tenaciously, he insists upon victory, utterly rejecting and renouncing the victim's role.

Men and women, boys and girls sit rapt, on the edge of their seats, as they hear him conclude his life story. His grammar isn't perfect. His diction isn't precise, but the power remains unmistakable. The challenge is irresistible, and the promise of astonishing victory is self-evident. It is personified in David Ring the evangelist—"one who brings good tidings."

He brings his testimony to a close with an unexpected performance.

> *There is a song I like to sing after my life story that sums up what I've been trying to say to you. I'm not a singer, I'm a preacher. God did not send me to sing, God called me to preach. And after I sing, you are going to say, "Amen. Stick to preaching, boy." But I love to sing this song.*
>
> *You say, "What key do you want it in?" I don't care. Pick one, because by the time we get finished, I'll be all over the keyboard.*
>
> *People, look at me. Look at me. Let this song bless you. I may not sing it well, but it is coming from my heart. Because you are looking at a man who has "Victory in Jesus."*

> > *I heard an old, old story,*
> > *How a Savior came from glory,*
> > *How He gave His life on Calvary*
> > *To save a wretch like me;*
> > *I heard about His groaning,*
> > *Of His precious blood's atoning,*
> > *Then I repented from my sins*
> > *And won the victory.*

O victory in Jesus, My Savior forever,
He sought me and bought me
With His redeeming blood;
He loved me 'ere I knew Him
And all my love is due Him,
He plunged me to victory,
Beneath the cleansing flood.

I heard about His healing,
Of His cleansing pow'r revealing,
How he made the lame to walk again
and caused the blind to see;
And then I cried, "Dear Jesus,
Come and heal my broken spirit,"
And somehow Jesus came and bro't
to me the victory.

O victory in Jesus, My Savior forever,
He sought me and bought me
With His redeeming blood;
He loved me 'ere I knew Him
And all my love is due Him,
He plunged me to victory,
Beneath the cleansing flood. *

* Words by Eugene M. Bartlett. © Copyright 1939 by E. M. Bartlett. Copyright 1967 by Mrs. E. M. Bartlett, renewal. Assigned to Albert E. Brumley & Sons. All rights reserved. Administered by Integrated Copyright Group, Inc. Used by permission.

David Ring Ministries is based in Franklin, Tennessee. David travels weekly to speak in churches of all sizes and denominations. He also often shares his message in schools, businesses, and civic organizations. His words of inspiration and of God's grace are being used to touch the hearts of thousands of people.

Audio- and videotapes of David's messages are available by mail, or by telephone with MasterCard or Visa. His story is told on a forty-five minute video presentation, "The Life Story of Evangelist David Ring," also available by telephone or mail.

You may contact David Ring Ministries at the following address and phone number when interested in scheduling a speaking date or ordering tapes.

David Ring Ministries
P.O. Box 682286
Franklin, Tennessee 37068
Phone: (615) 771-9600

Moody Press, a ministry of the Moody Bible Institute,
is designed for education, evangelization, and edification.
If we may assist you in knowing more about Christ
and the Christian life, please write us without obligation:
Moody Press, c/o MLM, Chicago, Illinois 60610.